G000152238

The Little Book of
piping quotations

The Little Book of
piping quotations

Stuart Letford

pipingscotland

Selected and edited by Stuart Letford

Published by piping**scotland**
www.pipingscotland.com

Copyright © piping**scotland**, 2004

Printed in Scotland

ISBN 0-9548830-0-4

Distributed by the College of Piping,
16-24 Otago Street, Glasgow, G12 8JH, Scotland, UK.
Telephone: +44(0)141 342 5252.

All rights reserved. No part of this publication may be reproduced, stored, or transmitted
in any form, or by any means, electronic, mechanical or photocopying, recording or
otherwise, without the express written permission of the publisher.

A Catalogue record of this book is available from the British Library.

Introduction

This little anthology concerns itself with piping – a rich source of material. The lack of a collection of piping quotations has been a glaring gap in the range of reference works that support us in the eternal quest of exploring what being a piper is all about.

For many, the Great Highland Bagpipe is more than merely a musical instrument: it is an embodied legendary epic. The late Robert Reid once said that piping was a disease; it could strike anywhere and was incurable. Moreoever, the late D.R. MacLennan recalled of his wild family of pipers that they were "not exactly what you would call religious. I suppose piping was their religion."

While there are quotes included that are about bellows-blown bagpipes, most concern the beast: the Great Highland Bagpipe. As David Murray put it, "None other can stir the blood, quicken the heartbeat, or move the soul as can the sound of the Great Music played on the Great Pipe, whether heard in a great hall or borne down the glen on the wind." And while there are quotes included that concern pipe bands, we nevertheless believe in the maxim that the only drums a piper needs to hear are 'heedrum' and 'hoedrum'.

Dugald MacNeill once quipped that it's "never too late to give up the bagpipe". However, we fear the quotes in this book show that, for many, once the piping bug has bitten it is unshakeable . . . like a disease, or, indeed, a religion.

Stuart Letford

Foreword

The bagpipe has been present at every momentous event throughout Scottish history, the battles which shaped its destiny, the celebrations and great occasions, and the sorrowing for the deaths of great heroes and famous people. For the individual Scot the bagpipe has marked the milestones in life. There are tales of being born to the sound of the pipe, married to it – either joyfully or, in the case of one lady, forcefully – and being laid to rest to its laments. For the exiled Scot, even at many generations distance, the bagpipe evokes images of Highland glens and lochs and the great deeds of the past.

For those presently involved in the piping world there are funds of stories about the great players of the past and these are constantly being augmented by the tales of present-day characters which will pass into folklore. The author of this book, Stuart Letford, has gathered together quotes covering all aspects of piping, and anyone with an interest in the history and music of Scotland will find something of interest here.

Jeannie Campbell

[The Great Highland Bagpipe] . . . hath no species of music peculiar to itself; and can play nothing which cannot be much better done upon other instruments.

__Encyclopaedia Britannica__ **(1778)**

The Return
(A Piper's Vaunting)

Och hey! for the splendour of tartans!
And hey for the dirk and the targe!
The race that was hard as the Spartans
Shall return again to the charge:

Shall come back again to the heather,
Like eagles, with beak and with claws
To take and to scatter forever
The Sasunnach thieves and their laws.

Och, then, for the bonnet and feather! –
The Pipe and its vaunting clear:
Och, then, for the glens and the heather!
And all that the Gael holds dear.

James Pittendrigh Macgillivray (1922)

The Heavyweights may be the glamour boys of the games and the arrival of the Chieftain may seem much grander but the true aristocrats of the Highland Games are the solo pipers.

Charlie Allan (1974)

The Games – A Guide to Scotland's Highland Games

'Ill-starr'd, though brave, did no visions foreboding
Tell you that gate had forsaken your cause?'
Ah! were you destin'd to die at Culloden,
Victory crown'd not your fall with applause:
Still were you happy in death's earthly slumber,
You rest with your clan in the caves of Braemar;
The pibroch resounds to the piper's loud number,
Your deeds on the echoes of dark Loch na Garr.

George Gordon, Lord Byron (1807)

Lachin Y Gair (Lochnagarr)

As the Highlands have been always the grand focus on insurrection here, from peculiarity of manners, idleness, and inaccessibility to the arm of the law, a language unintelligible to the more civilized districts, and other causes, so has the bagpipe been the concomitant of rebellion, as in Ireland.

Sir John Graham Dalyell (1849)

Musical Memoirs of Scotland (Edinburgh 1849)

From *Flora MacDonald's Love Song*

Allan, would that thou wert near me!
Allan donn, my dear, my treasure,
Heavy load of love I carry.
Allan, would that thou wert near me!

Harp nor fiddle e'er can lift it,
Nor shrill pipes with lilting chanter.
Allan, would that thou wert near me!

Sad, each day for thee I'm longing,
Gone with thee all joy and gladness.
Allan, would that thou wert near me!

In deep groves and leafy woodlands,
Fair would I with thee be wandering.
Allan, would that thou wert near me!

Allan of the curling ringlets,
Sweet to me thy honey-kisses.
Allan, would that thou wert near me!

Kenneth MacLeod (1927)

The Campbells are Coming is an arrangement of the Gaelic song *Baile Inneraora* or *Inveraray Town* which is anything but flattering to the Campbells. It was a march past of the 1st Bn. Argyll and Sutherland Highlanders, formerly the 91st Argyllshire Regiment, but the tune was anathema to the Cameron Highlanders, and earned instant loss of liberty for any piper rash enough to risk a few bars.

David Murray (1981)

Piping Times, July 1981

I'm a piper to my trade,
My name is Rob the Ranter:
The lassies loup* as they were daft,
When I blaw up my chanter.

Francis Sempill (c1655)

Maggie Lauder
* leap

one thing he had learned this afternoon:
playing the pipes was not a substitute for sex!

James Kelman (1989)

A Disaffection

A story was told me by a friend, of a Highland concert at which the chairman proclaimed that the proceedings were to be opened by pipe music played by a certain piper. Now the skill of this piper was not rated too highly locally, and he had scarcely taken the pipes from their box and walked on to the platform, when one of the audience, with more vigour than taste, yelled at the top of his voice, "Sit doon, ye _____." At once the chairman was on his feet and called out, in stern and disapproving tones, "Who called the piper a _____?" Came the answer instantly, in the broadest Scots, "Fa caa'd the _____ a *piper*?"

Seton Gordon (1947)

A Highland Year

Fame was worthily gained by Piper Findlater, from Turriff, who continued to blast out *The Cock of the North* although wounded in both ankles. This deed won for Findlater the Victoria Cross. Because of his wounds, Findlater was discharged, and finding his pension insufficient to support himself, was persuaded to re-enact his part in the battle on the music hall stage. A public outcry arose; the result was that the V.C. pension was increased.

David Murray (1981)

– on one piper's gallantry during the Gordon Highlanders' capturing of the Heights of Dargai in 1897. From the *Piping Times*, July 1981

Ach, man, everybody knows that when you leave the face of the note white it goes slow and 'Tiamhaidh, Tiamhaidh'*, and when you blacken her face she goes twice as fast, and when you tie her feet she goes twice as fast again, and the more you blacken her face and tie her feet the faster she goes, until she would leave Bran† himself behind her!

Pipe Major Niall Matheson (c1850s)

Pipers and Pipe Music in a Highland Regiment, by Major I. H. MacKay-Scobie – Matheson was being harangued by William Ross, Queen Victoria's piper, about staff notation. Many beginners would probably find his simplified explanation of musical theory very helpful!

---

* A Gaelic word meaning 'lovely, heart-melting' it is pronounced 'cheeavvy'.
† Bran was the swiftest deer-hound of Fingalian hero Cuchulain.

I honestly don't think that commercial interests interfere with the integrity of the judges. They have to be tested, and the end results . . . I know personally people have directed points of view to me, they have said, "Oh yes, when Shepherd judges, Shotts is first. When Shepherd judges another band that plays his chanters, they're first." This may be so, but I maybe only judge Shotts once in a year, and I always put the question, can you tell me why they shouldn't be first, or whatever? And they never seem to count the bands who get first from me who don't play chanters or reeds supplied by me. They always want to miss that.

Bob Shepherd (1997)

the Voice, Winter 1997

Bob Shepherd

A Glasgow Bagpipe Maker In Trouble

Early on Thursday morning in the shop of their father, a bagpipe maker in Royal Arcade, a quarrel arose between Robert MacKinnon, also a bagpipe maker, and Ronald MacKinnon, an engraver, in the course of which Ronald was stabbed with a knife in the groin and about the face, and seriously wounded. Ronald was removed to the Infirmary, where he still lies, and his brother is in custody.

Oban Times (1893)

". . . I'd like to know what you've been up to all this time you're supposed to be going to the well!"

"I was just looking at the sunset."

"Looking at the sunset, a chreutair! Looking at the sunset! Here's your faather no better than a slave the way he's working and you, ye sgalag, won't do a hand's turn. Ye should be ashamed of yourself, if you've any shame left in you. Going to the Univarsity this year an' ye can do nothing to help your faather for looking at the sunset! But that's what's wrong with ye! 'Worshipping the crayter more than the creator,' that's what's wrong with ye! If it's not the one thing it'll be the other you're at. Yesterday it was singing vain songs in Iain Beag's workshop. Last week your father goes over to Achgarve to Mary Bheag's Janet's wedding an' yonder's Murdo with an arm round a bag of pipes an' him blowing, yess, plowing like a – like a – like a whale, an' all the folk watching ye an' all. A fine like thing that for your faather's son! 'John the Elder's son's a piper,' they'll be saying. Och, it's myself can hear them saying it!

Fionn Mac Colla (1932)

The Albannach

. . . Later on I met Somerled MacDonald who had been judging, and enquired about the queer result. He, too, was 'ramping' and gave me the impression that he would have nothing to do with the decision. "The other two," he said, "said that George MacLennan was making false notes." This was a reference to the use of the G gracenote on the little finger movement which George MacLennan always played.

'Veritas' (1949)

– on the 1928 Northern Meeting.
From the *Piping Times*, January 1949. See Notes on p294

. . . *James Reid* was then tried, whom the Witnesses for the Crown plainly proved to have engaged with the rebels, and to have acted as a Piper to a Rebel Regiment, tho' it did not appear that he had ever carried any Arms; upon which he was recommended to Mercy by the Jury. The Court observed upon this, that every Person who joined any Set of People engaged in open rebellion, tho' they did not bear Arms, they were guilty of High Treason; that no Regiments ever marched without Musical Instruments, as Drums, Trumpets, or the like; and that in an *Highland* Regiment there was no Moving without a Piper, and therefore his Bagpipe, in the eye of the Law, was an Instrument of War. The Jury upon this would have retracted their recommendation, but the Court told them, it must not now be permitted – *Guilty*.

Unattributed (1746)

A True and Impartial Account of the Trials of the Rebels at York, (John Gilfillan 1746)
– Reid was executed. For an account of a piper who was more fortunate, see p264

The Pipers of Scotland may well be proud of the part they have played in this war. In the heat of battle, by the lonely grave, and during the long hours of waiting, they have called to us to show ourselves worthy of the land to which we belong. Many have fallen in the fight for liberty, but their memories remain. Their fame will inspire others to learn the pipes, and keep alive their music in the Land of the Gael.

Field Marshall Earl Haig (c1918)

Taken from *The Highland Pipe and Scottish Society 1750-1950*
by William Donaldson (Tuckwell Press 2000)

Had piobaireachd, which came to Nova Scotia as early as 1783 (Donald Rory MacCrimmon) survived – we would have a perfect experimental model for comparing music tradition in Cape Breton and Scotland. But the people came here without an army, without an empire to defend and without an aristocracy or even an upper class to act as patrons and cultural gamekeepers. What is amazing is that piping survived at all.

Professor Dan MacInnes (1998)

Piping Times, June 1998

He [Lord Lovat*] had all the atrocity of the oldest and most barbarous times. He began with the rape of his wife. He sent some of his banditti who set fire to Culloden House, the seat of President Forbes, who was his relation, and for whom he was at the same time professing the warmest attachment and regard. He had employed some of them to waylay and assassinate another relation, Sir Ludovic Grant, my father-in-law. In short, there was no outrageous villainy of which he was not capable. . . . All his behaviour previously to and at his execution evinced the perfect possession of his mind and even of gaiety. His conscience slept; or did he find some salve for its upbraidings in the idea of the wildness of the time and his character of Chieftain, indignant of rivalry and opposition? After all his atrocities, he died like a hero.

Henry MacKenzie (1824)

* Simon Fraser, Lord Lovat, was the last British peer to be condemned for treason. He was executed at the age of 80 for his part in the Jacobite rising of 1745-6.

He [6th Duke of Atholl*] was a living, a strenuous protest, in perpetual kilt, against the civilisation, the taming, the softening of mankind. He was essentially wild . . . he revived and kept up the games of the country, – the throwing the hammer, and casting the mighty caber; the wild, almost naked, hillrace; the Ghillie-Callum and the study of the eldritch, melancholy pipes, to which, we think, distance adds not a little enchantment.

Dr John Brown (1864)

* George Augustus Frederick Murray (1814-1864). He became Duke in 1864.

Calvinist Sang

A hunder pipers canna blaw
Our trauchled times awa,
Drams canna droun them out, nor sang
Hap their scarecraw heids for lang.

Gin aa the warld was bleezan fou,
What gowk wald steer the plou?
Gin chiels were cowpan quines aa day,
They'd mak, but never gaither, hay.

Pit by yir pipes and brak yir gless,
Wi quines, keep aff the gress,
The day ye need a hert and harns
Dour as the diamant, cauld as the starns.

Alexander Scott (1989)

trauchled – troubled; *hap* – cover; *fou* – drunk; *gowk* – fool;
cowpan quines – laying girls; *harns* – brains

The change from the heavy march, strathspey and reel in contests to the free selection has removed the necessity for pipers ever to play anything more difficult than "Highland Laddie." A few years ago all grades of bands except the lowest demanded that pipers should be able to play "Donald Cameron," "Blackmount Forest," "Bob of Fettercairn," "The Grey Bob" and such-like. Even the Boys' Brigade bands could play these tunes. Now when we do get a march, strathspey and reel contest, some of the top Grade 1 bands show that this standard is quite beyond them.

. . . We will view the demise of the free selection, or medley, with no trace of grief. The reason for which it was introduced was never valid, namely to provide better entertainment for the audience. The audience at a band contest cannot hear the performance properly in any case, so nothing will be lost and a great deal gained by changing back from ceol beag to ceol aotrom.

Seumas MacNeill (1976)

Piping Times, March 1976 (College of Piping)

After Dinner the Band played and two of my Company came and sang on the quarter Deck and they sang right well . . . the Band played after Mess also the Pipes and old McLean the Pipe Major danced and played the fiddle like a five year old.

Colonel John W. Wedderburn (1853)

– the 42nd returns home from Nova Scotia, 1852.

From *Highland Soldier 1820-1920* by Diana M. Henderson
(John Donald, 1989)

Illustration from a Second Scottish Poetry Book compiled by Alan Bold (OUP, 1985)
© Oxford University Press 1985, reproduced by permission of Oxford University Press.

The Bubblyjock

It's hauf like a bird and hauf like a bogle
And juist stands in the sun there and bouks.
It's a wunder its heid disna burst
The way it's aye raxin' its chouks.

Syne it twists its neck like a serpent
But canna get oot a richt note
For the bubblyjock swallowed the bagpipes
And the blether stuck in its throat.

Hugh MacDiarmid (1926)

*bubblyjock – turkey cock; bouks – hiccups; raxin' – stretching;
chouks – jaws; blether – windbag*

You've just murdered my uncle.

P.M. Angus MacDonald (2000)

– to a piper after hearing a bad rendition of his composition,
Alan MacPherson of Mosspark. From *Piping Times*, September 2000

The only place you'll see a well-dressed Border piper is on an undertaker's slab.

Jack Campin (2000)

Well played, watch those C doublings. I seem to be having a heart attack, would you please summon a doctor?

Iain MacPherson

– date unknown. Reader's letter, *Piping Times*, January 1996

Few instructions are necessary for those who commence playing the Highland Bag Pipe. The winding of the instrument or preserving an equal current of air, so as to produce a continuous sound is its chief requisite, and will be acquired by practice; the arm which supports the bag must be gently relaxed, as it is distended by the air blown into it, and the compressure will naturally succeed in the interval of taking breath.

The pupil must commence by holding up the drones with the hand which he intends to be the lower, at the same time seizing the chanter with the upper; the fingers should not be bent to cover the holes but placed straight over them, so that the notes B, C, & D, are covered by the first joints. The fingers should be raised high above the chanter that they may give the greater report in their fall: in blowing the pipes the cheeks must be firmly contracted, with a smile on the countenance.

William Ross (1869)

Ross's Collection of Pipe Music

Gordon Walker

William Ross

He plays before the laird every Sunday in this way to the kirk, which he circles three times, performing the family march . . . and every morning he plays a full hour by the clock, in the great hall, marching backwards and forwards all the time, with a solemn pace, attended by the laird's kinsmen, who seem much delighted with the music.

Mr Campbell himself . . . has an invincible antipathy to the sound of the Highland bagpipe, which sings in the nose with a most alarming twang, and, indeed, is quite intolerable to ears of common sensibility, when aggravated by the echo of a vaulted hall. He, therefore, begged the piper would have some mercy upon him, and

dispense with this part of the morning service. A consultation of the clan being held on this occasion, it was unanimously agreed, that the laird's request could not be granted, without a dangerous encroachment upon the customs of the family. The piper declared he could not give up for a moment the privileges he derived from his ancestors; nor would the laird's relations forego an entertainment which they valued above all others. There was no remedy; Mr Campbell being obliged to acquiesce, is fain to stop his ears with cotton, to fortify his head with three or four nightcaps, and every morning retire into the penetralia of his habitation, in order to avoid this diurnal annoyance.

Tobias Smollett (1771)

The Expedition of Humphry Clinker

The inn was shabby to the point of scandal, no better than a common tavern, smoke-blackened, smelling of the reek of peat and mordants used in dyeing cloth; lit by cruisies, going like a fair with traffic. In the kitchen of it men were supping broth with spoons chained to the tables, and a lad with his head to the side as if in raptures at his own performance stood among the ashes with a set of braying bagpipes.

Neil Munro (1935)

The New Road

Ass if it wassn't enough to have one fice itself it must be two or three or a dossen you have. One time it's bad books under the pillow, another time you're at the singing of fain songs, and now indeed it's the piping itself! And all this comes of the bad company you'll be keeping, yess, it's led astray you are by the keeping of baad company, and that's one of the Tefil's fayforite wayss of destroying the soul.

Fionn Mac Colla (1932)

The Albannach

. . . He seemed then to be convulsed; his pantomimical gestures resembled those of a man engaged in combat; his arms, his hands, his head, his legs, were all in motion; the sounds of his instrument were all called forth and confounded together at the same moment. This fine disorder seemed keenly to interest every one.

The piper then passed, without transition, to a kind of andante; his convulsions suddenly ceased; the sounds of his instrument were plaintive, languishing, as if lamenting

40

the slain who were being carried off from the field of battle. This was the part which drew tears from the eyes of the beautiful Scottish ladies. But the whole was so uncouth and extraordinary; the impression which this wild music made upon me contrasted so strongly with that which it made upon the inhabitants of the country, that I am convinced we should look upon this strange composition not as essentially belonging to music, but to history . . .

– Barthélemy Faujas de Saint Fond (1784)

– the French geologist's impressions of the 1784 Highland
Society of Scotland competition held in Edinburgh.

Bho *Am Pìobaire Dall*

Bu tu maighstir mòr na pìoba
a sheinneadh ruidhle no cumha,
's ged a bha thu dall nad shùilean
nad làimh bha fradharc dùbailt cubhaidh.

Ged a bha thu dall nad shùilean,
bha gibhtean dùbailt' nad mheuran:
chluinneadh An Sìthean Mòr port tiamhaidh
's bhiodh na sìdhichean tinn le iadach.

Chitheadh tu le do sprùdan
ged a bha do shùilean gun sholas:
bu mhòr na dealbhan bhiodh a' dannsa
nuair dhòrtadh meall den cheòl bhod chorraig.

Maoilios Caimbeul (2002)

From *The Blind Piper*

You* were the great master of the pipes
who could play a reel or a lament,
and although your eyes were blind
your hands were justly double visioned.

And although your eyes were blind,
your fingers were double gifted:
the great fairy knoll would hear a plaintive tune
and the fairies would be sick with envy.

You had digital vision
although your eyes were dark:
many's the picture would dance
when a shower of music would pour from your fingers.

Myles Campbell (2002)

* John MacKay, the Blind Piper of Gairloch (c1656-1754)

I have before me a large amount of piobaireachd music written in Staff Notation with every vocable written below the appropriate note, which is the work of Simon Fraser of Australia. By this work, Simon Fraser, in my opinion, has . . . to be considered as an authority on the subject, both by his superior settings and skill in noting. I have conclusive proof that the settings used by Fraser were noted direct from John Dubh [MacCrimmon].

Pipe Major William Gray (1951)

Oban Times, February, 1951
See Notes on p292

Little Birds are playing
Bagpipes on the shore,
Where the tourists snore:
'Thanks!' they cry. ''Tis thrilling.
Take, oh, take, this shilling!
Let us have no more!'

Lewis Carroll

– date unknown

Gay pipes of the sticks smooth
And heads of bone,
Hard wood of Jamaica growth.
The best there were grown;
Lathe-turned, and round, and straight,
Ivory-tinged,
Mouthpiece, chanter, all ornate,
With sweet sound winged.

Duncan Bàn MacIntyre (c1760)

It is probably safe to say that never before has this classical piece [*MacCrimmon's Sweetheart*], full of melody and difficult to express except by the highest exponents of piping, been played in unison by two pipers, but so perfectly did MacDonald and Reid play that it seemed as though only one pipe was heard sounding over the hills and over the sea.

Seton Gordon (1933)

– from his report in *The Times* on the unveiling of the MacCrimmon cairn at Boreraig, Skye, on 2nd August, 1933

John MacDonald, Inverness, and Robert Reid playing at the MacCrimmon cairn

I had gone to this gathering knowing nothing of an unfortunate, although perhaps amusing, difference between the pipers and the management. On my arrival, William McLennan met me and asked me what the devil I was doing there.

I replied that I was not afraid of any of them, and asked why I should not be there.

He explained that they had protested against the smallness of the prizes, and that they were not going to play.

I replied that I had paid for my return ticket to Inverness, and was going to play. Eventually Angus Macrae and [John MacDougall] Gillies played, although they had protested, but [John] MacColl and MacLennan did not. They got into some trouble for booing those who played. Gillies got the piobaireachd and I was second. The judges praised my playing but for my reed. Someone had removed my own reed and substituted another.

Robert Meldrum (1940)

Oban Times, July 1940.

When a chief goes a journey in the hills, or makes a formal visit to an equal, he is said to be attended by all or most part of the officers following, viz.:–

The henchman.
The bard or poet.
The bladier or spokesman.
The gillemore, bearer of the broadsword.
The gillecasflue, to carry the chief when on foot over the fords.
The gille comstraine, to lead the chief home in dangerous passes.
The gille trusharnish or baggage man.
The piper, who, being a gentleman, I should have named sooner. And lastly,
The piper's gillie, who carries the bagpipe.

There are likewise some gentlemen near of kin who bear him company, and besides, a number of the common sort, who have no particular employment, but follow him only to partake of the cheer.

Unattributed (1716)

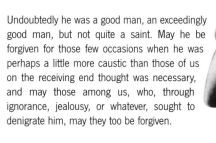

Undoubtedly he was a good man, an exceedingly good man, but not quite a saint. May he be forgiven for those few occasions when he was perhaps a little more caustic than those of us on the receiving end thought was necessary, and may those among us, who, through ignorance, jealousy, or whatever, sought to denigrate him, may they too be forgiven.

Dugald MacNeill (1996)

– speaking at the service of remembrance for Seumas MacNeill and quoted in the *Piping Times* of May 1996

Seumas MacNeill

From *Tam o' Shanter*

. . . And, wow! Tam saw an unco sight!
Warkocks and witches in a dance:
Nae cotillion, brent new frae France,
But hornpipes, jigs, strathspeys, and reels,
Put life and mettle in their heels.
A winnock-bunker in the east,
There sat Auld Nick, in shape o' beast;
A tousie tyke, black, grim, and large,
To gie them music was his charge:
He screw'd the pipes, and gart them skirl,
Till roof and rafters a' did dirl . . .

Robert Burns (1791)

unco – wondrous; *brent* – brand; *winnock-bunker* – window-seat; *tousie tyke* – shaggy dog; *skirl* – squeal; *dirl* – ring

© National Museums of Scotland

The Piobaireachd is now, and has been for many years, in a dilapidated condition, mainly through the introduction of "Sitirichean an Eich – Raoichden as Asail agus geumnaich a Mhairt" (the neighing of the horse, the braying of the ass, and the lowing of the cow),

The Horse   **The Ass**   **The Cow**

together with unqualified men writing music they knew little or nothing about, thereby making bagpipe playing a variety of wild and meaningless notes, as if Momus, the god of mockery, was trying his best to show the piper as a full-grown clown.

John MacLennan (1907)

Preface *The Piobaireachd As Performed In The Highlands for Ages Till About The Year 1808* by John McLennan (John MacLennan, 1907)

The first time I heard piobaireachd . . . I was crying and crying. It was wonderful. It gave me a feeling I sometimes have from sacred music. Piobaireachd seems like a mantra, a spiritual thing, that moves you deeply. I think if you don't want to listen to your soul, if you are afraid of your deep side, you hate piobaireachd. I think it can take you into your true self.

Daniela Ballardini (2004)

Piping Today

. . . Lieut. MacCrimmin's present residence is in Kirktoun, near Bernera barracks, Glenelg. When I called, I found that he was at his farm in Glenbeg, a *long mile's* distance from his present place of abode. I had little time to spare and, rather than await his home-coming, I set out to find him. And on my coming to the spot, I found him leading in his corn with the assistance of some neighbours of his own name, amongst whom he is a sort of Chieftain. He is upwards of '*three-score and ten*': rather thin, stoops a little – is about the middle size – has all the appearance of having been in his earlier years handsome.

. . . As I had come such a distance to hear him perform on his fvourite instrument, and converse with him concerning the theory & practice of the Great Highland bagpipe, he sent for Alexander Bruce, Piper of Glenelg, a favourite pupil of his own, who played several pieces in a stile of excellent, that while it excited applause, reflected much credit on his able Preceptor, who encouraged him occasionally with approbation.

After a few good glasses of his own good toddy, MacCrummin seized the pipe – *put on his hat* (his usual custom) – breathed into the bag – tuned the drones to the chanter – gave a prelude in a stile of brilliancy that flashed like lightning, and commenced FAILTE

PHRIONNSAH*, in tones that spoke to the ear, and affected the heart. Thro' the whole of this fine *Salute*, he shewed a masterly command of the instrument; – the manner in which he moved his fingers seems peculiar to himself, the effects he produces by this means are admirable – there is not a sound lost – not the quickest appoggiatura, how rapid soever the movement or the variation – and the regular return to the subject or *theme* of the piece, is in fine contrast with the more intricate passages. Are the talents of MacCrimmin doomed to decay in solitude?

Alexander Campbell (1815)

---

* *The Prince's Salute*

Mhic Mhoire na gréine,
A ghiùlain do cheusadh,
'S tu m'aighear is m'eudail 's mo threòir.

Greas thugainn dhachaidh
Oighre dligheach na h-aitribh,
Nam pìob is nam brataichean sròil.

Eachann Bacach (c1650)

Son of Mary, Lord of the sun,
who hast suffered crucifixion,
Thou art my joy, my treasure and my strength.

Send home speedily to us the lawful heir of the house,
the man of the pipes and the satin banners.

Eachann Bacach (c1650)

From Iorram to Sir Lachlann, a song in
praise of Sir Lachlann MacLean of Duart

Sir, – I am obliged to 'Another Celt' for his intelligent letter of the 26th inst. I now understand that the *performer* is at fault, and that the ancient piobaireachd is a thing of the past. This is surely a lamentable state of affairs, and I am sure all lovers of our national music will regret it. Are there no means by which we can resuscitate these tunes so that they may be played and appreciated as they have been in the past? The piobaireachd books without exception are full of errors, some of them most glaring; but surely there are some intelligent men who could put a musical construction on these compositions, and at least save them from being the laughing stock of nations. I am, etc.,

'Celt' (1893)

Oban Times, September 1893

– 'Celt', according to William Donaldson, *may* have been Dr Charles Bannatyne, a 'gentleman amateur, who was a frequent correspondent to the *Oban Times* on piping subjects. He was subsequently an advisor to the Piobaireachd Society.

Imagine the leading violinists and pianists, if they had to perform at 9.30am on a September morning in the Highlands, their shelter nothing but a small roof, which in no way prevents rain, snow or a piercing wind reaching them, paralysing their fingers and playing the very mischief with those reeds that for weeks past they have been coaxing into condition. Added to the vagaries of the weather from which they suffer, they are lucky if their music is uninterrupted by the screech of a passing train or the explosion of a pistol within a few yards distance. the patience of the modern piper might well be as proverbial as that of Job. But what of the audience? Perhaps no hall could be found large enough to contain those Highlanders who talk glibly and with so little knowledge of their national instrument. They

are not present. The grand stand is empty. Away in the open you will find a small crowd, among them a few who will hang on every note – an old piper or two listening with the appreciation of the true artist as the clear notes of a great pibroch swell upon the air, denoting the touch of a master hand. To gain applause for piping, it is better to collect a dozen indifferent pipers, as many drums as possible, and let them go round playing some trivial march with no great respect for tune or accuracy. Then with satisfaction the audience will proceed to congratulate themselves on their Highland music, while the genuine musician is only longing for a grateful pause of silence.

Editorial, *Oban Times* (1920)

I remember hearing a young boy playing away by himself and putting in wonderful taorluaths in *The Piper's Bonnet*. When he stopped we approached and asked his name. He replied simply, "George MacLennan." Shortly afterwards we heard him give one of the finest exhibitions in the march competition with *Abercairney Highlanders*, but he did not appear on the prize list. When we went to offer our consolation later, he said that the judges had thought he had put too much work into the tune, and, had added, that didn't worry him as his father had told him he would win prizes some day. His father was perfectly correct.

Archibald MacNeill (1948)

– recalling Luss Highland Games c1896

G.S. MacLennan, aged 10

60

. . . I forgot to tel yu yt the Duc of Perth, who as I told yu before, acted no more as General officer, desired the Prince's leave to go to Perth, with thirty or forty gents yt were willing to follow him, & bring the Prince, with the greatest dilligence he cou'd, the troops yt. were at Perth. He lay at Kendal; the next morning, two of his servants yt stayed behind, were surrounded by the Mob, & almost murd'red, & were oblidged to stay there, one of them I fancy dyed of his wounds . . . The men, who were informed of what happened [to] the Duke of Perth, were resolved to be revenged of the town, breaking open houses, shopes, takeing all they cou'd find in 'um, in short comitting all the mitchchief they cou'd. The Prince nor the Chiefs, cou'd find no other means to appease the disorder but by getting the pipers plaid, to assemble the men, to make a general revew, wch scheme succeeded & very much apropos, for about the time yt they were under armes, we had an acct that the enemy was near at hand . . .

John William O'Sullivan (1747)

1745 And After by Alistair and Henrietta Tayler.
– O'Sullivan was one of the 'Seven Men of Moidart' who landed with Prince Charles Edwart Stuart at Loch nan Uamh on 25th July, 1745.
See Notes on p292

The pipe reed obeys no laws. Like the most fickle woman, it rewards, if at all, the lavish attentions of an honest heart with but a brief and transient display.

J. C. M. (1949)

Piping Times, October 1948

Reed-making is a most particular industry, and its secrets are jealously guarded. The less the writer says on this subject, the better his chance of living to a good old age.

James Robertson (c1930)

from *The Highland Pipe and Scottish Society 1750-1950* by William Donaldson (Tuckwell Press 2000)

And wild and high the 'Cameron's gathering' rose!
The war-note of Lochiel, which Albyn's hills
Have heard, and heard, too, have her Saxon foes:-
How in the noon of night that pibroch thrills,
Savage and shrill! But with the breath that fills
Their mountain-pipe, so fill the mountaineers
With the fierce native daring which instils
The stirring memory of a thousand years,
And Evan's, Donald's fame rings in each clansman's ears!

Lord Byron (1812)

– on the Battle of Waterloo
Childe Harold's Pilgrimage

Nature hath fram'd strange fellows in her time. Some that will evermore peep through their eyes and laugh like parrots at a bagpiper.

William Shakespeare (c1596)

The Merchant of Venice, c1596

. . . He says to my father. Tormod Mor. Ookie, he says. For our breakfast in Fort Cheorge we got a haraag hard tack biscuit *nach tarraing thu null* you wouldn't give to a haraag mangy dog. *Nach toir thu dhomh rum.* And a cup of cold tapwater. *'S a' fuachd ann.* Them was the days, Ookie. Tormod Mor said. And marching to the sound of the bagpipes. Cound't march the same to a brass band. Or Mendelssohn. Couldn't keep the step. Wee Donald Macleod was Pipe Major in Fort George. Had Shakespeare heard Wee Donald Macleod on the bagpipes, he'd have changed his opinion of the instrument.

Alasdair Campbell (2003)

– from *Visiting the Bard and Other Stories* (Polygon)

From *North of the Tweed*

And yet you mind, dear, on the bridal hill
Hoo yon laich loch ootshone my een in yours,
Nor wi' the heather could oor bluid compete,
Nor could the ring I gie'd you when your hand
Lay on the crucifers compare wi' them
Save for a second when the sun seized on't.
Hair of the purple of Strathendrick Hill,
Slant e'en wi' pupils like blue-stane washed wi' rain
And the whites owre white and the hunted look
Here tak' your bairn; I've cairried it land eneuch,
Langer than maist men wad, as weel you ken.
Noo I'll pipe insteed – what tune'll you hae? –
On Rudha nam Marbh.*

Hugh MacDiarmid (1930)

Selected Poems

laich – low; *insteed* – instead;
* The Point of the Dead

The MacDougalls and Stradivarius lived in different worlds, if not separated by time, yet both had this in common; firstly, they were perfectionists in the art of music, and secondly, they were experts in the art of wood-turning. If there is such a thing as the perfect musical instrument, then the MacDougalls and Stradivarius by combining the two arts came close in their time to achieve that aim.

Unattributed (c1911)

A Hollow On The Hill
by Nancy Black, July 1999

This day Abigail Crombie, ane randy wha stoppit in the Canongate forenent Baldy Longmuir's alehouse, declarit before my Lord Kindrouthy and ithers, that she could blaw upon the pipis baith louder and langer and mair wyslyk nor ony Hielant kerne that never wore breekis. Whereupon, pipis being brocht till hyr scho did blaw intil thalm sae michtily that hyr braith gaed clean frae hyr, in sicwyse that the skin o' hyr wame flappit back agin hyr backbane and thair stickit: sae that she fell down and would have deeit had not auld carle namit Sandy Cheyne, wha keepit ane brazier on the whilk he roastit chestnuts for the callants o' Heriot's, gruppit haud of hys bellows, the whilk he stikkit straightways intil hyr mou, and sae did blaw hyr up again.

The Scotsman (1748)

Translation – This day Abigail Crombie, one riotous, belligerent, dissipated beggar who stayed in the Canongate beside Baldy Longmuir's alehouse, declared before my Lord Kindrouthy and others that she could blow upon the pipes both louder and longer than and more wiselike than any lazy or slovenly Highlander that never wore trousers. Whereupon on pipes being brought to her she did blow into them so mightily that her breath went clean from her, in suchwise that the skin of her wame flapped back against her backbone and there stuck: so that she fell down and would have died if had not an old man named Sandy Cheyne, who kept a brazier on which he roasted chestnuts for the young people of Heriot's, gripped hold of his bellows which he stuck into her mouth and did blow her up again.

The Piper o' Cargill

Tam Tupp the piper o' Cargill
(There's been nae better piper)
Aince fund a puddock in the well
And taucht it monie a caper.

Ae nicht what Tam was lauchin fou
He gied the beast a jorum;
And cried: "Come on, my puddle-doo,
We'll hae the Tullochgorum."

There's aye some ferlie on the earth;
But maist are happ't and hoddie:
And at Cargill, no far frae Perth,
Tam's yirded wi' his puddy.

William Soutar (c1930)

aince – once; *puddock* – a frog; *ferlie* – a wonder

The Mad Music

There was mad music came through the glen,
And it cast a spell on our strong young men,
And they left the croft, and they left the mill,
And the sheep at the shearing out on the hill,
And, without a sigh or a backward look,
They took the road that the pipers took.

When the mad music came through the glen,
There was never a lad for a sweetheart then.
What is the tune that the pipers played
With a stronger charm than the smile of a maid?
And what is the dream that the young men dream
That lights their eyes with that strange glad gleam?

Oh! the same tune rang through the glen of yore;
''Tis the pibroch's call to war, red war.
And the dream is as old as the world's story,
For the dream is the old, old dream of glory.
Oh! the mad music came through the glen
And carried away our strong young men.

W. D. Cocker (1914)

Poems, Scots and English

. . . his back got sore and he shifted his position and let his eye wander over the bens and the loch and the while houses of Sand and Badachro shining through the heat-mist at the far side of it. Life must have been good here in the old days, with a song never far from the lips and feet ever itching to be at the dancing. And the fine piping there must have been! But then the dark days came, with a new kind of religion that changed the old ways, stopped the song on the lip, and let the wind out of the pipes with a squealing of the drones. Then the folks began going abroad till none were left but the old people and bairns.

Fionn Mac Colla (1932)

The Albannach

I've only flirted with it [piobaireachd] over the years and would never claim to know very much about it, and I'm always suspicious of people who tell me they do know a lot about it. I think there is an awful lot of romanticism attached to it and most of the performances of piobaireachd that I've heard I would say that the player's usually enjoying it more than the listener.

Robert Mathieson (1988)

The Piper Press, January 1998

They put me in the toilets for a while to learn how to play the way they played. It was very intensive and a very good grounding

Gordon Mooney (1986)

– recalling joining the famous Muirhead & Sons Pipe Band.
From *Common Stock*, the journal of the Lowland & Border Pipers' Society, 1986

The bagpipes are not an instrument for women, and indeed, are equally unsuitable for men, except for those poor wretches who are paid to play them and make a trade of it.

Giovanni Della Casa (1558)

I saw that Pipe Major Grant was very drunk. He made a most horrible noise on his Pipes and as the men were all laughing, I told him when near the Casemate Barracks to leave off playing – which he did. Naturally as a young Subaltern – I held the Pipe Major in great reveration and I was determined to say nothing more and let him walk to barracks if his legs would take him there. However when we got into the most crowded and narrow part of the Gibralter main street he suddenly slipped off down a side street and disappeared.

General Sir Spencer Ewart (1882)

– quoted in *Highland Soldier 1820-1920*
by Diana M. Henderson (John Donald, 1989)

All concerts and parties generally ended with a ball and the numerous Friendly Societies springing into existence required fiddlers to play in their yearly processions, and accompany the toasts with appropriate music. On these occasions tarns of whisky and toddy disappeared with the usual "Here's to ye," and eternal friendship was vowed under the influence of an evaporating spirit. Customs like these in time told on the musicians, and too often was fiddler and piper synonymous with intemperance.

John Cuthbert (1881)

Crieff: Its Traditions and Customs
by D. Macara

From *A Lament for Corrienessan*

"A blessing to you and victory in battle
everywhere you take your playing
for the sake of your tune, eloquent and hearty,
while the sun goes down in the evening.

That is the music of the sweetest sadness
heard since the time of Donald MacKay*;
for a while yet in my ears it will linger,
that swift playing from your fingers."

Blind John MacKay (1697)

* Donald *duaghal* MacKay, 1st Lord Reay

As long as there's humanity and as long as there's bagpipes, people are still going to be moved by the great Highland bagpipe, whether they have any connection with it or not. It's survived all these years because of what it is."

Eric Rigler (2004)

Piping Today, issue 11, 2004

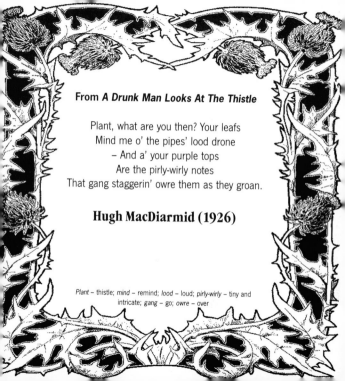

From *A Drunk Man Looks At The Thistle*

Plant, what are you then? Your leafs
Mind me o' the pipes' lood drone
– And a' your purple tops
Are the pirly-wirly notes
That gang staggerin' owre them as they groan.

Hugh MacDiarmid (1926)

Plant – thistle; *mind* – remind; *lood* – loud; *pirly-wirly* – tiny and
intricate; *gang* – go; *owre* – over

. . . there is his *hanchman*, or right-hand man, then his *bhaird*, or poet; then his *bladier*, or orator, to make harangues to the great folks whom he visits; then his *gilly-more* or armour-bearer, to carry his sword, and target, and his gun; then his his *gilly-casflue*, who carries him on his back through the sikes and brooks; then his *gilly-comstraine*, to lead his horse by the bridle in steep and difficult paths; then his *gilly-trusharnish*, to carry his knap-sack; and the piper and the piper's man, and it may be a dozen young lads beside, that have no business, but are just boys of the belt to follow the laird, and do his honour's bidding.

Walter Scott (1814)

– from *Waverley*, where Ewan Dhu tells Edward Waverley of the accompaniments of a chief

One day the priest lifted a solemn finger before his nose and began fumbling in an inside pocket of his coat. With a face of portentous gravity he drew out a silver-mounted chanter, adjusted the reed and fitted it together. Then he began playing, while Murdo tapped time with his toes, inside his boot. When he had finished the little reel he played he handed the chanter over the Murdo, who played another, the priest tapping on his knee with plump fingers and clearly delighted. They were there at the piping, laments, reels and marches and snatches of piobaireachd, sitting forward in their chairs as eager as schoolboys and the feadan passing between them until in the middle of a tune the priest happened to look at the clock, and he was up on his feet, clapped his hat on his head and skipped out of the room with the feadan still in his hand almost before Murdo realised the music had stopped.

Fionn Mac Colla (1932)

The Albannach

From *The Arrows of Glen Lyon*

Lord of Sronmilchon,
unless I am mistaken,
is the title which fittingly honours you.

Poet bands praise you,
journeying for provisions,
your purse was always prepared for them.

Beer in tassies,
being drunk by nobles
whatever the hour we visited.

Pipes inciting,
wine outpouring,
men with long tressies at backgammon.

Unknown (c1603)

– a MacGregor leader is being praised as he prepares to leave for battle, possibly to Glen Fruin. Taken from *The Harps' Cry* (Birlinn, 1994)

. . . Not that the professional competitor is one to be sneered at or held up to reproach in any way. On the contrary he is a man who should be appreciated. He is bustled by pompous stewards. He is put on a platform to play amid the din of a brass band and the hooting of steam merry-go-rounds . . . He is frequently the victim of cruel injustice at the hands of ignorant judges. Yet he takes a multitude of annoyances, which might tempt him to commit a breach of the peace, invariably with the characteristic good humour and cheerfulness with which he is endowed.

Pipe Major William Gray (c1950)

– from his handwritten notes, which were without title or date but appear
to be for a lecture to the Scottish Pipers Association

Shakespeare's play of Blood and Death,
Gave Scots the wicked Lady MacBeth;
But could she dance a Highland Fling,
Or even some Ceol Meadhonach sing?
If you look up your Donald MacPhee,
On page thirteen you plain will see,
"MacBeth's Strathspey" (no word of Sadie),
Then pray sir, where do you find the "Lady"?

D.R. MacLennan (1956)

Piping Times, April 1956.
– the *P.T.* ran a series on readers' popular tunes and one submitted
<u>Lady</u> *MacBeth's Strathspey* instead of *MacBeth's Strathspey*.
This was D.R. MacLennan's reply.

From *Song to Dòmhnall Gorm Og, MacDonald of Sleat*

To the hall of cups
where wine-quaffing makes din,
where a thousand bets are concealed.

A harp and a clarsach
and fair-bosomed women
in the tower of the short gaming boards.

The blasting of bagpipes
and Leith organs
with drinking horns filled to the brim;

Wax blazing
all through the nighttime,
as they listen to the contention of bards.

In the hall of the grandson
of the Earl of Islay,
of the Hebrides, Kintyre and Ross.

Iain Lom (c1643)
– see Notes on p293

Kenny Mhurchaidh Bhig cleared his throat, "What tune is at you there?"

Murdo put the name on it.

"O-ho," says Kenny, in a mocking tone. "There now! That's *just* what it will be, right enough. And who taught you it like that?" he added with something like venom.

"It was my mother taught me," replied Murdo, smiling with a corner of his mouth.

"Well, it was a worthy woman that was in your mother," says Iain Beag, turning himself round and if anything smiling a little too. "But she had it wrong. Here to me the feadan."

Kenny Mhurchaidh Bhig snorted and rammed his thumb into the bowl of his pipe. Iain Beag was on the point of putting the feadan to his mouth when the door opened a little and the face of Duncan Lachlan Iain appeared squinting round the edge of it.

"It was with me that I was hearing the birds of spring and they singing in winter," says he, coming in. "In the name of God what have I here?"

"Were you not thinking it was MacCruimein himself you were hearing?" says Kenny Mhurchaidh Bhig.

He got up wearing his spitting face. Murdo stepped hastily aside from the vicinity of the fire.

"Indeed, I was thinking it was MacCruimein," says Duncan. "And if I thought I thought also that it was the rheumatics that were in the finger-joints of the worthy man." He winked his good eye at Murdo.

"Well, apart from yon trifling error about MacCruimein you were nearly right, for it was the rheumatics the woman had that taught him the tune." Kenny ran his eye with lingering scorn down Murdo's person.

"God about us!" exclaimed Duncan Lachlan Iain, as if in the greatest consternation. "A woman piper! I won't believe it. The day I see a man bear a child that day I'll see a woman tune the pipes, and that day I'll know am dead. Man, man, they have not the wind nor the trick of the fingers nor the musician's ear nor the poet's heart."

Iain Beag smiled a little at the man's fervour and Murdo had difficulty in keeping back the grin that came natural to the face of one that would be conversing with Duncan Lachlan Iain.

Fionn Mac Colla (1932)
The Albannach

I have been requested by some pipers to answer the question. Did John MacCrimmon use the low A in Taorluath and Crunluath as written by D[onald]. MacDonald, Angus MacKay, and other writers of Piobaireachd. Most certainly he did. I know this beyond any doubt. Those pipers who do not play the low A have not been properly taught, and it is a great pity that they are trying to lead other pipers astray.

Simon Fraser (1929)

Oban Times, November 1929
– taken from *The Highland Pipe and Scottish Society, 1750-1950*,
by William Donaldson (Tuckwell Press, 2000). See Notes on p292

. . . He jumped to his feet and took the pipes from the old man's hands, and over his shoulder with the drones.

"Stand back, lad!" he cried to Gilian, and Gilian went nearer the door.

The march came fast to the chanter – the old tune, the fine tune that Kintail has heard before, when the wild men in their red tartan came over hill and moor; the tune with the river in it, the fast river and the courageous that kens not stop nor tarry, that runs round rock and over fall with a good humour, yet no mood for anything but the way before it. The tune of the heroes, the tune of the pinelands and the broad straths, the tune that the eagles of Loch Duich crack their beaks together when they hear, and the crows of that countryside would as soon listen to as the squeal of their babies.

Neil Munro (1896)

The Lost Pibroch

Bho *Fuaim an Taibh*

Re fuaim an taibh
'S uaigneach mo ghean –
Bha mis uair nach b'e sean m'abhaist,

Ach pìob nuallanach mhòr
Bheireadh buaidh air gach ceòl
Nuair ghluaiste i le meòir Phàdraig.

Màiri nighean Alasdair Ruaidh (c1641)

From *The Ocean's Sound*

At the ocean's sound
my mood is forlorn –
not always has feeling thus been my custom,

But a great roaring pipe
that left all music behind
when it was stirred by Patrick's fingers.

Mary MacLeod (c1641)

– the exiled bard addresses Sir Tormod MacLeod of Berneray (d. 1705). Taken from *Gàir nan Clàrsach* (Birlinn, 1994). See Notes on p295

The piper stretched his right hand above his head, feeling backwards, and touched tenderly with a finger the drones. His hand remained a moment in the air and a listening came into his puckered face as he lent a careful ear to their roaring. Then he took off the high note he had been holding on the chanter and, still listening, broke a handful of chattering notes, preliminary. someone burst into merry laughter and clapped his palms together, making a noise that flew upwards and exploded under the roof like a ball of hollow sound. The loud noise of many people talking, moving about, guffawing and laughing, fell suddenly to a sibilant ripple round the walls. Attention became fixed on the erect figures in the middle of the room, poised, waiting. With a movement of his right hand the piper pressed the bag upwards under his oxter, and fell at once into the tune. Twenty-four young men and girls, as one person, began to dance.

    . . . This night since the dropping of dark the sound of dancing and merriment had come from the lighted building above the high road. The sense of accustomed restraints so lately loosed brought an edge and an abandon. The pipes roared through the room, buffeting the ears. An excitement gripped the breasts and mounting upward like a heady vapour looked out in shining eyes. Not only the dancers whirled and danced but the blood throbbed in time in wrists and temples and glowing cheeks. Nothing went that was not in time. Even through the minds the long thoughts did not pass nor the odd-shaped fellows, and but the half-thoughts tripped it, sharply, pleasant, on the feet of the reel. They were yonder in a kind of intoxication, drunken with sound and a wild defiance of the music. In the meekest breast an ancient affirmation raised its head; the dullest understood an antique something, stirred obscurely at the core.

Fionn Mac Colla (1932)

The Albannach

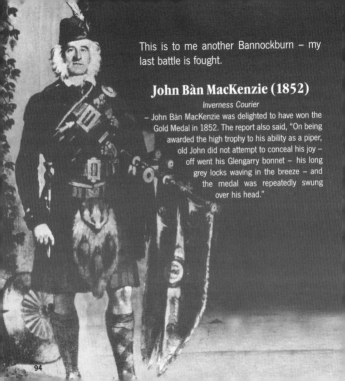

This is to me another Bannockburn – my last battle is fought.

John Bàn MacKenzie (1852)

Inverness Courier

– John Bàn MacKenzie was delighted to have won the Gold Medal in 1852. The report also said, "On being awarded the high trophy to his ability as a piper, old John did not attempt to conceal his joy – off went his Glengarry bonnet – his long grey locks waving in the breeze – and the medal was repeatedly swung over his head."

Sir, – . . . In reply to the inquiry of your correspondent whether there are any MacDonalds who can still trace back their ancestry to Glencoe, I may inform you that the 'Big Piper' who played on the night of the massacre, was my grandfather's great-grandfather. He escaped on the night of the massacre. Being a powerful man he ran towards the river Coe which at that time was frozen over. The soldiers fired a volley after him; but though it did not take effect he himself fell upon the ice, and the soldiers seeing that he did not move, returned. He made his escape to the Pap of Invercoe, and remaining there all night, found his wife and family next morning among the frost and snow.

'Clachaig' (1894)

Oban Times letters page, September 1894

The Pap of Glencoe

The Praise of the Bagpipes

Woe to the one who decries music and war-march,
to mighty heroism inciting hosts;
great pipe that inspires all courage
her noise, the more terrible for its beat.

I love the harp, my great love the pipe,
I abominate the one who it decries;
no sense of obligation is poor reward for music,
the deaf ear of a poet busy with verse.

I am not about to dispraise verse,
for verse would be all right at time of peace;
but verse never affected her foes
anything as deeply as did the pipe.

If you were to see me on a slope
under a banner of red and white,
better a blast from the pipe for an hour
than all the poetry between here and the grave.

Sweet to me the sound of her drones
gathering armies under her skirts:
if a poem chanced to come under her cloak
she would feel better off in Hiort!

The sweet-worded woman with never a rotten huff,
gentle smooth-worded, and that is no lie,
who speaks softly in every mode,
on a man's shoulders her kerchief thrown.

The standard greatest for rallying hosts,
to decry it finally is woe.

Woe to the one who decries.

Gilleasbaig of Keppoch (c1670)
– see also p103 and Notes on p292

By and by, the day being worn on to afternoon, I hear a distant Noise of Bag-pipes which grows ever louder, then I espy men a-moving down Glen-Spean from the east. Looking at 'em through the Glasse, I see that these are Clans-men, in Blue Bonnets and Belted Plaids, each with a Round Buckler and girt Sword, some with Muskets or Halberts besides; some there be a-horseback in glitt-ring Panoplie of gold-laced Coat, Breastplate and plumed Helmet, these I take to be their Chiefs.

Aphra Behn (1689)

Aphra Behn – Dispatch'd from Athole. The Journal of
Aphra Behn's Secret Mission to Scotland in 1689.
Transcribed by Ross Laidlaw (Balnain Books, 1992)

Inverlochy Castle

From *Mac Neachdainn's Song*

Whosoever met with you in conflict,
indeed he was soon defeated.
With you the Gordons would rise faithful,
the troops with the shod, grey horses;
numerous their pikes in bundles,
numerous their pipes and banners,
numerous their guns and helmets,
numerous their bows and straight arrows,
numerous their precious dirks and pistols,
numerous the toledos at their left-sides,
in a quiver of yew in a hide cover.

Unknown

– a song in praise of a MacNaughton chief. Taken from *Gàir nan Clàrsach* (Birlinn, 1994)

. . . Claverhouse drew his sword, and the light of the West ran along the blade like bright water as he brought it up in the signal to charge.

"Forward in the King's name! God be with the right!"

The cheering ran along the line from the MacLeans at one end into the shadow of Creag Eileich at the other, and was lost in the bright yelping of the bugle and the sudden wild crying of the pipes that seemed to leap up from the heather as the crying of the whaups leaps skyward. And the line moved forward.

Rosemary Sutcliff (1983)

Bonnie Dundee

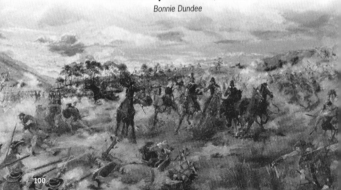

Saturday, November 16 – The Duke of Perth proclaimed King James, attended by the Mayor and civil officers in their robes, with their sword and mace. The keys of the city were presented to the Prince at Brampton by the Mayor and Corporation on their knees; and on Monday the 18th His Royal Highness made his entry into Carlisle seated on a white charger and preceded by not less than 100 pipers.

Lord George Murray (1745)

– writing to his brother William, the eldest son of the
first Duke of Atholl and known as Duke William
(*Chronicles of the Atholl and Tullibardine Families, vol III*)

This is not a wee foray of broken men, but an attack by an army of numbers . . . I doubt MacCailein Mor heard little of this uncheery criticism, for he was looking in a seeming blank abstraction out of the end window at the town lights increasing in number as the minutes passed. His own piper in the close behind the buttery had tuned up and into the gathering –

"Bha mi air banais 'am bail' Inneraora.
Banais u mhiosa bha riamh air an t-saoghal!"

I felt the tune stir me to the core, and M'Iver, I could see by the twitch of his face, kindled to the old call.

Neil Munro (1898)

John Splendid

Inveraray Castle

Reply to *The Praise of the Bagpipes*

My lifelong curse, Gilleasbuig,
on your pithless body,
because, over all the world of music,
you gave first place to the pipe.
Players of stringed instruments
often had to listen to your abuse, and you repaid them badly:
yet you were the man to eat bread and puddings and meat,
you lousy churl!

Many an earl in Scotland tonight,
lying farting in his bed
having filled his belly with sowens from the pot,
and developing flatulence,
would gladly, for hearing her [the pipe] night and morning
(they would find it distasteful to give her any respect),
reward the confusion of her drones
by setting the dogs on it.

Lachlann Maclean (c1715)

– see p96/97 and Notes on p292

On a sudden there rose away before us towards the mouth of the glen the sound of a bagpipe. It came on the tranquil air with no break in its uproar, and after a preparatory tuning it broke into an air called Cogadh no Sith – an ancient braggart pibroch made by one Macruimen of the Isle of Sky [sic] – a tune that was commonly used by the Campbells as a night-retreat or   tattoo . . . it roused in me spirit very antique, very religious and moving too, as the music of his own land must in every honest Gael.

"Cruachan for ever!" I said lightly to M'Iver, though my heart was full.

He was as much touched by that homely lilt as myself. "The old days, the old styles!" said he. "God! how that pibroch stings me to the core!" And as the tune came more clearly in the second part, or Crunluadh as we call it, and the player maybe came round a bend of the road, my comrade stopped in his pace and added with what in another I might have thought a sob – "I've trudged the world; I have learned many bravadoes, so that my heart never stirred much to the mere trick of an instrument but one, and the piob mhor conquers me. What is it, Colin, that's in us, rich and poor, yon rude cane-reeds speak so human and   friendly to?"

"'Tis the Gaelic," I said, cheered myself by the air. "Never a roar of the drone or a sob of the chanter but's in the Gaelic tongue."

Neil Munro (1898)

John Splendid

I maintain that a Highlander incapable of discerning the beauties of a piobaireachd through all its faults has been, in his education, deprived of half his birthright.

General C. S. Thomason (1894)

From *The Massacre of the Macpherson*,

Fhairshon swore a feud
Against the clan M'Tavish;
Marched into their land
To murder and to rafish;
For he did resolve
To extirpate the vipers,
With four-and-twenty men
And five-and-thirty pipers.

W E Aytoun (c1930)

Our company had but one piper and he was not provided with arms and the usual means of defence like the rest of the men as to keep aloof for safety. When our line advanced the charge, General Townshend observing that the Piper was missing, and he knowing well the value of one on such occasions, he sent in all directions for him and he was heard to say aloud, "Where's the Highland Piper?" and "Five pounds for a piper," but de'il a bit did the Piper come forward. However, the charge by good chance was pretty well effected without him as all those that escaped could testify. For this business the Piper was disgraced by the whole of the Regiment and the men would not speak to him, neither would they suffer his rations to be drawn with theirs, but had them served out by the commissary separately and he was obliged to shift for himself as well as he could.

Sergeant Thompson (1759)

– taken from *Traditional Gaelic Bagpiping 1745-1945*
by John G. Gibson (NMS Publishing, 1998).

Cumha na Cloinne
(The Lament for the Children).

Urlar.

In spite of the wonderful visual and tactile sensuousness of much seventeenth-century and still more of eighteenth-century Scottish Gaelic poetry . . . I think that, on the whole, the Scottish Gael is more fascinated by sound in poetry than by visual form or colour. At any rate, I do not think that there is any doubt that the greatest glories of Scottish art are in the great pibrochs, such as *The Lament for the Children* . . .

Sorley MacLean (1991)

Preface, *From Wood to Ridge*

On one occasion a company of the Gordons were marching from a place called Jullunder to Fort Kangra, situated on one of the lower ranges of the Himalayas. Accompanying them was an elephant, on which were placed sick and exhausted men. After a few days' march they were deprived of music on account of the piper's feet becoming blistered, and he was relegated to the back of the elephant. On the last day's march, before entering their new station, someone suggested that in order to brighten them up the piper might be requested to play on the elephant's back at the head of the company. To this the officer assented, and accordingly the piper was handed his pipes. When he began to tune them up it was evident that the elephant had no appreciation of such sounds, for he shook his head, flapped his big ears menacingly, raised his trunk, with which he embraced the piper round the waist, and violently threw him and his pipes into a ditch as a mark of his disapproval of such music.

W.L. Manson (1901)

The Highland Bagpipe

He [John MacDonald, Inverness] was without doubt the kindest of men, one of the finest players and teachers of Piobaireachd, and the most cantankerous old B_____ that ever lived. Nobody's best was ever good enough. Pipe Major Donald MacLeod was taking lessons from him at the same time, and he fared no better than I. However, I must hold the record, as he told me once, after struggling through a Piobaireachd, 'That is the worst tune I have ever heard in my life'.

Hamish Mackenzie (1998)

Piping Traditions of the North of Scotland,
by Bridget MacKenzie (John Donald, 1998)

John
MacDonald

Bho *Cochur*

Nighean, a nighean mo luaidh,
b' e aoibhneas a' chiùil mhòir t' aodann,
Beethoven agus Maol Donn
air magh lom cridhe sgaoilte.

. . . Thachd an fhiabhrais ioma truagh
is dh' fhàg i ioma athair breòite,
ach dh' fhàg ceòl cumha Phàdraig Mhòir
àmhghar a chloinne glòrmhor.

. . . Cha dèanar an cochur dhe 'n chas,
glòir agus ànradh na cruinne,
an eitig fhiabhrais 's Pàdraig Mòr,
daorsa, Beethoven is thusa.

Somhairle MacGill-eain (1938)

From *A Synthesis*

Girl, girl of my love,
the joy of the big music was your face,
Beethoven and Maol Donn
extended on the bare plain of a heart.

. . . Fever has choked many a poor one
and has left many a father bruised, sore and frail,
but the music of Patrick's lament
left the distress of his children glorious.

. . . No synthesis will be made of fortune,
the glory and the distress of the universe,
the feverish wasting and Patrick Mor,
slavery, Beethoven and you.

Sorley MacLean (1938)

– verses 6, 10 and 13

I have been playing pipes for 39 years, and in all these years I never heard a whisper that the open C was wrong until recently. Before the last war I was a very successful competitor for years around the Highland games and wherever piping competitions were held, Glasgow included. Would you believe it – the judges, rather than tell me that my open C was wrong and sounded awful and thereby give away the secret, actually gave me prizes instead, even first prizes. Now doesn't that beat cock fighting? My own teacher, the late Roddie Campbell, never breathed a word to me about my C being wrong; in fact, he was always very careful to play the open C himself in my presence.

. . . When I am judging piping, I never take marks off a man because he plays an open C.

John Wilson (1954)

Piping Times, August 1954

Sir, – If you will protect me I will write about drumming and piping... But I have fears for my life. Drummers are terrible fellows, and if my name and hiding place were revealed they might come and drum near me, and I would soon die of old age . . .

'MacVourich' (1925)

Oban Times, February 1925

Television interviewer: "Why should people learn to play the bagpipe?"
Seumas MacNeill: "So that they don't waste their time watching television."

Piping Times (1959)

The Clan Chisholm preserves, or at least did at one time preserve a relic believed to be of great antiquity. It is a chanter which is supposed to have a peculiar faculty of indicating the death of the chief by spontaneously bursting, and after each fracture it is carefully repaised by a silver fillet, which is an improvement on the original method of mending with a leathern thong. The family piper, when from home at a wedding, heard his chanter crack, and at once started up, saying he must return, for The Chisholm was dead. And he was.

W.L. Manson (1901)

One of the pipers I remember coming to our house to play for us was Duncan Campbell, the ploughman at Oskamull. He was nicknamed 'the Duke' for no better reason, as far as I knew, than that he was a Campbell. Like the great pipers of old he gave a name to his pipes – he called her Lucy. Lucy was a temperamental creature that demanded much attention before each performance . . . at length when Lucy's demands were satisfied the Duke would begin to play, marching up and down the cement floor . . . not that he always succeeded in completing the tunes, Lucy's tantrums intervening. Then the Duke, modest, not to say self-deprecatory to a fault, would say, "Chan eil agam ach criomagan." ("I have only fragments.") He never blamed Lucy.

Donald W. MacKenzie (2000)

Sin Mar a Bha, As It Was
(Birlinn, 2000)

Coronach for the End of the World

Like them or no' you canna deny
If you think the maitter owre
The Pipes are the only instrument
To soond Earth's mortal hour.

They should be keepit for that you think?
The joke may pass but yet
A fittin' fareweel to a' that's been
Is nae ither wise to get.

Mony a piper has played himsel'
Through battle and into daith,
And a piper'll rise to the occasion still
When the warld is brakin', faith!

A trumpet may soond or harps be heard
Or celestial voices sweet,
But wi' nocht but the cry o' the Pipes can Earth
Or these – or silence – meet.

The Pipes are the only instrument
To soond Earth's mortal hour;
But to greet what follows, if onything does,
Is no' in even their power.

Hugh MacDiarmid (1933)

They are always attired in the Highland costume of the house of Stuart, and accompanied by a piper of the clan. They have never worn any other dress than the kilt and its Highland appendages, and their seal is a crown. At the time they embarked* the piper played some of the principal Jacobite airs, composed as laments at the misfortunes of the Pretender.

The Times (1836)
– see Notes on p293

*The Sobieski brothers were departing Greenock to visit Ulster.

When man first fand the want o' claes,
The wind and cauld to fleg,
He twisted round about hims waist
The tartan philabeg.

And music first on earth was heard
In Gaelic accents deep,
When Jubal in his oxter squeezed
The blether o' a sheep.

The braw bagpipes is grand, my frien's,
The braw bagpipes is fine;
We'll teuk another pibroch yet,
For the days o' auld lang syne.

Unknown (1891)

– to the tune of *Auld Lang Syne*

Bho *Craobh nan Teud*

An clàrsaich Ruari
's am piob nam Pàdraig
tha craobh ghràidh mo luaidhe,
an luasgan Phàdraig
tha àilleachd luathghair,
ceòl suaimhneis àlainn,
an ceòl geal gàireach,
ceol gràidh mo luaidhe.

Somhairle MacGill-eain
(c1940)

From *The Tree of Strings*

In the harp of Ruairi
and the pipes of the Patricks
is the loved tree of my talk
in Patrick's unrest
is the paean beauty,
the serene lovely music
the white crying music
the music of my love and talk.

Sorley MacLean
(c1940)
From Wood to Ridge

. . . Unlike Lucy, the Duke's demands were very modest – frequent and copious cups of strong, sweet tea. From time to time throughout the course of an afternoon, he would indicate his need for refreshment with a set phrase – "Tha pàthadh searbh orm." (There is a bitter thirst on me). Tea, long stewed with milk and sugar was the the essential accompaniment of all the social gatherings in the home where stories were told, songs sung and pipes and fiddles were played. To provide it was to pay a very modest price for the pleasure the performance gave us . . .

Donald W. MacKenzie (2000)

Sin Mar a Bha, As It Was
(Birlinn, 2000)

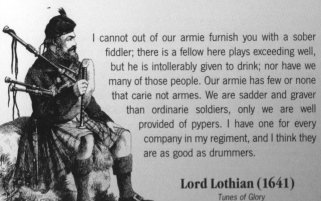

I cannot out of our armie furnish you with a sober fiddler; there is a fellow here plays exceeding well, but he is intollerably given to drink; nor have we many of those people. Our armie has few or none that carie not armes. We are sadder and graver than ordinarie soldiers, only we are well provided of pypers. I have one for every company in my regiment, and I think they are as good as drummers.

Lord Lothian (1641)
Tunes of Glory

We played *Donald MacLean's Farewell to Oban, Dorrator Bridge* and I think the set finished with *Over the Isles to America*. We thought we were the best band there, but the band that won it was a made-up band. Extra pipers used to get a good drink in them, and five or six of them would get together and go out to the field as a band. The fact that they had no drummers didn't matter . . . that's the way it was in those days.

Maclean Macleod (1998)

– recalling a typical American Highland Games of the 1960s.
From *the Voice*, Spring 1998

From *A Drunk Man Looks At The Thistle*

You canna gang to a Burns supper even
Wi'oot some wizened scrunt o' a knock-knee
Chinee turns roon to say, 'Him Haggis – velly goot!'
And ten to wan the piper is a Cockney.

Hugh MacDiarmid (1926)

scrunt – person whose growth is stunted or emaciated;
knock-knee Chinee – music-hall caricature of a Chinaman

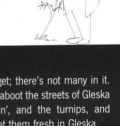

And good pipers iss difficult nooadays to get; there's not many in it.
You'll maybe get a kind of plain piper going aboot the streets of Gleska
noo and then, but they're like the herrin', and the turnips, and
rhubarb, and things like that – you don't get them fresh in Gleska.

Neil Munro (1906)

The Vital Spark

126

Highland games gave visible shape to class-based division between competitors and sponsors, between those who performed and those whose superior social standing entitled them, with varying degrees of competence, to judge. The games represented two opposite, and ultimately irreconcilable, impulses: while at the forefront of the new mass popular entertainment market in a rapidly modernising country, they were dedicated at the same time to proclaiming the values of a characteristically rural and hierarchical order. The apparent object was entertainment. The real agenda was about deference and social control.

William Donaldson (2000)

The Highland Pipe and Scottish Society 1750-1950 (Tuckwell Press 2000)

Monument to King George
IV's visit to Edinburgh, 1822

Cock o' the North, my Huntly bra',
Where are ye wi the Forty-twa,
Ah! waes my heart that ye're awa',
Carle, now the King's come!

But yonder come my canty Celts,
With durk and pistol at their belts,
Thank God, we've still some plaids and kilts,
Carle, now the King's come!

Lord, how the pibrochs groan and yell,
MacDonell's tae'en the field himsel',
MacLeod comes brankin' o'er the fell,
Carle, now the King's come!

Walter Scott (1822)

Carle, now the King's Come!
– on King George IV's visit to Edinburgh
in August, 1822

At the final of the Knockout competition in Glasgow both contestants displayed the deliberate false fingering which, if continued, will be a nail in the coffin of our noble instrument. The winner was the man who did it least – in fact hardly at all. The gimmicks were apparently enjoyed by a large number of the audience, but it has to be remembered that most of the audience were probably there to support one or other of the contestants. Also most of them did not appear to be Highland pipers. If this kind of fingering reached the final by popular acclaim then obviously these were the people who wanted to hear more of it.

Seumas MacNeill (1993)

Piping Times, July 1993

It is ironic that the best evidence available to prove the existence of the legendary MacCrimmons derives from a certified lunatic, who thought he was married to Queen Victoria, strenuously believed that Prince Albert was defrauding him of his marital rights, and was considered by the leading psychiatrist of his day to be "the most violent patient in England", with a predeliction for enticing people to approach him, then punching or kicking them in the testicles.

Alistair Campsie (1980)

The MacCrimmon Legend – The Madness of Angus MacKay by Alistair Campsie
(Canongate, 1980)

. . . G.S. McLennan was doing that long ago! [bending notes and false fingering] I actually played many years ago at the ceilidh after the Glenfiddich, and played *The Little Cascade*, and other tunes with false notes and smears and his family was there. D.R. McLennan came over to me and said, "That's not new, sonny."

Robert Mathieson (1997)

The Voice, Autumn/Fall 1997

Bho *An Cuilithonn*

Air Sgurr Dubh an Dà Bheinn
Thàinig guth gu m' chluais a' seinn,
Pàdraig Mór 's a cheòl ag caoinneadh
Uile chlann a' chinne daonna.
Agus feasgar air a' ghàrsbheinn
Bha ceòl eile ann a thàining,
Maol donn agus ùrlar sàth-ghaoil
A' bristeadh cridhe nam fonn àlainn.

Somhairle MacGill-eain (1939)

From *The Cuillin*

On Sgurr Dubh of the Two Hills
a voice came to my ear singing
Patrick Mor and his music mourning
all the children of mankind;
and an evening on the Garsven
there was another music that came,
'Maol Donn' and its theme of love-fullness
breaking the hearts of lovely tunes.

Sorley MacLean (1939)

From Wood to Ridge

. . . Her Majesty and Prince Albert, accompanied by Lord and Lady Glenlyon, then walked in front of the brave clansmen of Athole, made almost a military inspection of their appointments, and expressed great admiration of their appearance and seeming tact; they afterwards walked for some time on the lawn, affording spectators a view of their persons, and acting so graciously, that each individual in the assemblage might almost have fancied himself a particular object of their attention. A perpetual strain of the national music streamed from the bagpipes, and awoke echoes among the woods during the whole period of Her Majesty's stay; and it was accompanied, for some time, by the performance on the part of the Hon. James Murray and other select Highlanders, of the strathspey and Highland reel, and the celebrated national dance over two claymores. Her Majesty was so delighted with this performance, and with all the details of her reception here and over the previous parts of her route, that she now expressed to the Duke of Buccleuch the probability of her early repeating her visit to Scotland.

W.J. Hooker (1844)

Aeneas Rose, Pipe Major of the Atholl Highlanders from 1860-90. He was great-uncle of P/M Willie Ross

. . . In dramatic contrast to the Duke and his beloved Lucy was another piper and his pipes who visited us in summer. This was Pipe Major William Gray of the City of Glasgow Police Band, one of the most distinguished pipers of the 1920s and 30s . . . [He] used to spend his summer holiday at Oskamull farm with the MacFadyens – Mrs MacFadyen, Katie MacGregor before marriage, was, I believe, related to him. We could hear him play of an evening outside the farm, the music carrying clearly and sweetly over Loch-a-Tuath. He would spend an afternoon with us at the manse – a well set-up man, dressed in a tweed plus-four suit, with a genial affable manner, playing his magnificent, full silver-mounted bagpipes that, unlike Lucy, appeared to perform perfectly without the need of any cosseting.

Donald W. MacKenzie (2000)

Sin Mar a Bha, As It Was (Birlinn, 2000)
– see Notes on p292

From *I Am Minded to Rise*

I am minded, minded, minded,
I am minded, minded, minded,
I am minded, minded, minded,
I am minded to rise.

That's the well-judged toast,
Let's drink it cheerfully,
The toast of Allan of Moidart:
It's my wish for you to rise

Though you might be far from us,
My mood and spirits would revive
When I heard the news I wanted most
Of the warrior of the exploits

When the evening would darken
Lively would the young men be,
Great pipes would be incited there
And chanters being tuned.

John MacDonald (c1715)
– see Notes on p293. Taken from *An Lasair* (Birlinn, 2001).

I have always been a diehard in scouting the theory that every good thing in this island must have been invented somewhere else, and in asserting ceol mor to be wholly a Highland product. Arguing with me once on this point Douglas Ramsay propounded an interesting theory. A piobd, he said, is akin to a sonata. It may be going too far to say that piobd was invented where the sonata was invented – but two facts are significant. i) the sonata is 'heavy stuff'. ii) Both piobd and sonata end with 'fireworks'. All genuine native British music, English, Irish, Scottish & Welsh is tuny melodious stuff. There is no British 'heavy stuff' except piobd. Thus piobd may be a Highland invention but the germ of the idea came from abroad, probably from Austria.

Archibald Campbell

– date unknown. Quoted in *Piobaireachd and its Interpretation*
(John Donald, 1987)

Seumas MacNeill: Duncan, you are one of our better pipers and you do not compete. Why?

Duncan Johnstone: Och, I don't enjoy competing, anyway I don't think you play at your best when competing.

Seumas: Nonsense. Up on the platform that's when you really are at your best.

Duncan: No, No, when you're playing away in the kitchen that's when you are at your best. No strain, no tension.

Seumas: Not at all. On the platform with the adrenalin running brings out the best. Anyway you've never heard me playing in the kitchen.

Duncan: No, I've heard you on the platform and that's bad enough.

Seumas and Duncan (c1968)

Piping Times, December 1996
– the two had been preparing to record the "Chanter" piping programme at the BBC studios in Glasgow, and were asked to chat away so the technician could get a balance.

A Song to Red Allan

In the dusk of the evening
There was burning of brandy,
French wine you'd be quaffing,
Waxen candles being lit,
Some great chief would encourage your music,
Some great chief would encourage your music.

Revealed would be a fiddle,
Pleasant company on dance-floor,
Bagpipe sounding the chanters,
Sound of hall in the background
Playing games with young men's bandoleers,
Playing games with young men's bandoleers.

The youth's my joy and my treasure,
The cheerful sensible Allan
Who was heroic and learned,
Who grew up brisk and respected,
I found joy in your court, and not sadness,
I found joy in your court, and not sadness.

Niall MacMhuirich (1716)

– verses 6, 7 and 8. *An Lasair* (Birlinn, 2001). See Notes on p293

The Black Book of Clanranald

Competitions are the things that drive excellence for a lot of people. If there weren't competitions we wouldn't have the level of excellence we do. And the bagpipe, more than most instruments, is one of those instruments that, in order to produce the music, you have to have a level of technique which is very high. The idea of pipers who are musical but not technically strong probably doesn't exist.

Colin MacLellan (2004)

Piping Today

Her Majesty the Queen having directed that the Regiment *on all* occasions march past to the Pipes, this will take effect from this date. When marching past the Pipes will fall in in front of the Band.

Unattributed (1871)

Permanent Order Book, 91st (1st Battallion, Argyll & Sutherland Highlanders)

I first met Donald Cameron more than 30 years ago, and though I was the pupil of his brother Alexander, and met them both again when home on furlough in '61 and '62, strange to say I could not get Donald to play for me. The only explanation that was ever offered me for this was that Donald knew my anxiety, even then, to book all that came within my reach as regards Ceol Mor, and he had a horror of any "chiel takin' notes". Then even more than now very few pipers could write down what they heard – I myself was a beginner at that art – and possibly Donald dreaded the results of inaccurate reporting. He had no real education himself, and scoffed at the idea of anyone presuming to write down from ear.

General C. S. Thomason (1906)

Oban Times, September 1906

Bho *Moladh Chabair Féidh*

Faire, faire, 'shaoghail –
Gur caochlaideach carach thu!
Chunna mis', a Shìophort
Nam pìob cruaidhe sgalanta,
Nach robh an Alb' a dh'aon-shluagh,
Ged shìneadh Mac Cailein ris,
Na cumadh riuts' an eudann
Nuair dh'éireadh do chabar ort.
Ch'éireadh leat an còir 's an ceart
Le trian do neart, gu bagarach,
Na bh' eadar Asainne 's fa dheas
Gu ruige Sgalpa chraganach,
Gach fear a' glacadh gunna snaip,
Claidheamh glas no dagachan –
Bu leat Sir Dòmhnall Shléibhte
Nuair dh'éireadh do chabar ort.

Dh'éireadh leat fir Mhùideirt
Nuair rùisgte do bhrataichean:
Le'n lannan daite dùbhghorm

Gun ciùirrte na marcaich leo;
MacAlastair 's MacFhionghain
Le'n cuilbheirean acfhainneach,
Nuair rachadh iad san iorghaill
Gum b' iongnadh mur trodadh iad.
Bidh tu fhathast gabhail aighear
Ann am Brathainn bhaidealach –
Bidh cinneadh t' athar ort a' feitheamh,
Có a bhrathadh bagradh ort?
Bidh fion ga chaitheamh feadh do thaighe
'S gur lìonmhor pìob ga gleusadh
Nuair dh'éireas do chabar ort!

**Murchadh MacMhathain no
Tormod Bàn MacLeòid (c1716)**

From *In Praise of Chabair Féidh*

So that's how it is, O world –
How fickle and changeable you are!
I have seen, O Seaforth
Of the fierce sounding pipes,
That there was no tribe in Scotland,
Even if in bed with Mac Cailein,
Who'd hold up their face to you
When your antlers rose over you.
There'd rise with you in right and justice
With a third of your strength, threateningly,
All between Assynt and the south
And away out to rocky Scalpay,
Each man seizing a firearm,
A grey sword or a little gun –
Sir Donald of Sleat would be with you
When your antlers rose over you.

The Moidart men would rise with you
Wen your banners were unfurled:
With their stained blue-black blades,

They would wound the cavalry;
MacAllister and MacKinnon
With their efficient culverines,
When they joined a battle
It's unlikely they wouldn't fight.
You will once again be cheerful
In battlemented Brahan –
With your father's kin attending you,
Who would dare to threaten you?
Wine will be drunk all over your house
And many pipes will be tuned
When your antlers rise over you!

Murdoch Matheson or Norman MacLeod (c1716)

– the last two stanzas. This satirical poem was written by either Murdoch Matheson from Kintail or Norman MacLeod from Lochbroom. It concerns the 1715 Jacobite Rising. Taken from *An Lasair* (Birlinn, 2001).

It was, as is well known, customary for neighbours to visit each other's houses nightly, and to while away part of the long winter evenings, in reciting tales and traditions, singing songs, or playing some musical instrument. Now, all this is completely given up . . . It is rare to hear a song sung, and still rarer to hear the sound of pipe or violin.

Rev. Archibald Clerk (1841)

New Statistical Account, Durinish (Isle of Skye) parish entry

Loch Roag, Isle of Skye

When he [Bob Nicol, right] took you through a tune, he was so clear on it. There were no fuzzy parts at all. It was like he gave you the path through the woods, and it was up to you to take the path. A lot of people feel that he was intolerant of things being done any way but the way he showed you. Actually, he wasn't intolerant, but he was very clear on what he presented. He would often say, "I've given you the bones of the tune, now you put the flesh on it."

Donald Lindsay (1999)

the Voice, Spring 1999

. . . As soon as the victory was assured, the victorious army moved off towards Limerick, leaving the vanquished to bury their dead. Alasdair's* funeral was to Clonmeen, on the opposite bank of the Blackwater, where he was buried in the family plot of Donough O'Callaghan . . . It is possible to follow the route of the sad cortège through the little boreens, to visit the ruined chapel and somewhat jumbled graveyard; no stone preserves the name or memory, but it takes little imagination to picture the scene of lamentation as this youthful hero was laid to rest, a mere 27 years of age. It is said that a pibroch, *MacAllistrum's March*, was played at the funeral, as it had been played before the battle, and that for 200 years it remained current in Munster, with the human voice serving instead for the drone of the pipes.

Kevin Byrne (1997)

Colkitto! (House of Lochar, 1997)

---

* Alasdair MacCholla, youngest son of Colkitto MacDonald, was murdered by one of his captors after the Battle of Knocknanoss, near Cork, in November 1647.

From *The Praise of Gairloch*

Although I've been travelling the Lowlands
I don't care much for them at all,
Though I'm down here my good wishes go
To the people who're calm and not miserly;
When the daylight runs out you'll come from the ebb
To the limewashed room of the cups –
The music of chanters with John inciting it
Will be there to make light of your sorrows.

A full bowl upon table will be awaiting them
To cheer the spirits of the company,
A ballad will go round whose worth could not be heard
By the heroes who've toured around Europe;
There will be waulking and work-song, ballad and rowing song
And a skilful set from the *Òinsich*
For the splendid company of the wounding weapons
Who are brave in the army of battle.

William Ross (1783)

– see Notes on p294

Scott Monument,
Edinburgh

It appeared to be very generally thought, when the first programmes were issued, that the Highlanders, their kilts, and their bagpipes, were to occupy a great deal too much space in every scene of public ceremony connected with the King's reception. With all respect and admiration for the noble and generous qualities which our countrymen of the Highland clans have so often exhibited, it was difficult to forget that they had always constituted a small, and almost always an unimportant part of the Scottish population; and when one reflected how miserably their numbers had of late been reduced in consequence of the selfish and hard-hearted policy of their landlords, it almost seemed as if there was a cruel mockery in giving so much prominence to their pretensions.

John Gibson Lockhart (1837)

The Life of Walter Scott
– Lockhart expresses his reservations on his father-in-law's stage-managing of the Royal Visit to Edinburgh in 1822

John MacDonald used to tell me that, from my playing of 'Patrick Og', he suspected that it must be my favourite tune. Unlike Kilberry*, I do not have a favourite tune in piobaireachd or in any other classical music. If forced to settle for just one of each, I think they would be *The Lament for the Earl of Antrim* and Beethoven's *Archduke Trio*. But I think I do have a favourite composer – Iain Dall MacKay, the celebrated blind piper . . . In some parts of this tune [*The Lament for the Laird of Anapool*], if the player is not thinking at least two bars ahead he may fail to convey the beauty of Iain Dall's somewhat intricate phrasing of this fine melody. Hector Berlioz was described as a great inventive genius, and so was Iain Dall MacKay.

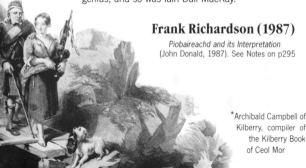

Frank Richardson (1987)

Piobaireachd and its Interpretation
(John Donald, 1987). See Notes on p295

*Archibald Campbell of
Kilberry, compiler of
the Kilberry Book
of Ceol Mor

It was a custom, very lately abolished, for the highland lairds to be attended by their pipers wherever they went. A laird in Morven had taken his piper with him to the funeral of a deceased friend: when the corpse was committed to its native dust, a banquet was prepared in the church, and after the glass had circulated pretty freely, the laird ordered his piper to strike up, who, being as ready as his master, strutted up and down the church, making it resound with his melodious strains: at last he placed himself upon a tombstone, and played several airs: this so provoked a descendant of the person who was interred under the piper, who thought it an insult to the manes of his ancestor, that he went behind the musician, drew his dirk, thrust it into the wind-bag, and effectually stopped his pipe.

Thomas Garnett (1811)

Tour through the Highlands and Part of the Western Isles, 1811

A chanter without a sole is a chanter without a soul.

P/M John MacKenzie (c1960)
The Piper Press, No. 7

The bagpipers, three in number, screamed, during the whole time of dinner, a tremendous war-tune; and the echoing of the vaulted roof, and clang of the Celtic tongue, produced such a Babel of noises, that Waverley dreaded his ears would never recover it. Mac-Ivor, indeed, apologised for the confusion occasioned by so large a party, and pleaded the necessity of his situation, on which unlimited hospitality was imposed as a paramount duty. "These stout idle kinsmen of mine," he said, "account my estate as held in trust for their support; and I must find them beef and ale, while the rogues will do nothing for themselves but practise the broadsword, or wander about the hills, shooting, fishing, hunting, drinking, and making love to the lasses of the strath. But what can I do, Captain Waverley? everything will keep after its kind, whether it be a hawk or a Highlander."

Walter Scott (1814)

Waverley

Among the Scots Highlanders, the chief gave a great entertainment after any successful expedition, to which all the country round was invited. On an occasion like this, the whole deer and beeves were roasted, and laid on boards or hurdles of rods placed on the rough trunks of trees, so arranged as to form an extended table, and the uisge-beatha went round in plenteous libations. This was called the *slige-creachain* from being drunk out of a shell. The pipers played during the feast, after which the women danced, and, when they retired, the harpers were introduced.

James Logan (1876)

A Handbook of the Scottish Gaelic World by Michael Newton
(Four Courts Press, 2000)

Dined at Mess at 7 O'clock. The Band and Pipes played. The first quickstep the Pipes played did not seemingly please Col. Cameron who ordered them never to play it again, poor Ross the Pipe Major was horribly disgusted as it happened to be a first rate tune . . . I at once rose and left the mess table in a rage.

Col. John W. Wedderburn (1847)

Highland Soldier 1820-1920 by Diana M. Henderson
(John Donald, 1989)

A wild cry of joy from the advancing battalions rent the air, and was then lost in the shrill clangour of the bagpipes. as the sound of these, in their turn, was partially drowned by the heavy tread of so many men put at once into motion. The banners glittered and shook as they moved forward, and the horse hastened to occupy their station as the advanced guard, and to push on reconnoitiring parties to ascertain and report the motions of the enemy. They vanished from Waverley's eye as they wheeled round the base of Arthur's Seat, under the remarkable ridge of basaltic rocks which fronts the little lake of Duddingston . . . When Waverley reached that part of the column which was filled by the clan Mac-Ivor, they halted, formed, and received him with a triumphant flourish upon the bagpipes, and a loud shout of the men, most of whom knew him personally, and were delighted to see him in the dress of their country and of their sept.

Sir Walter Scott (1814)
Waverley

Edinburgh Castle

To me, it is as futile to ask why drone reeds double-tone as it is to ask why a baby cries. Both are demanding attention, possibly because they are having wind troubles or their

bridles are too tight, or they need to be wetted or are too wet, but usually they both do it out of sheer malice, to test their owner's moral fibre.

J. A. C. Fisher (1970)

Piping Times, September 1970
(College of Piping)

It is said of John Bàn [MacKenzie] that he was the last of the old school, who with his own hands could kill the sheep, and fashion the bag, and turn the pipe, and cut the reeds, and compose the tune, and play it – with equal facility.

William Donaldson (2000)

The Highland Pipe and Scottish Society, 1750-1950, by William Donaldson (Tuckwell Press, 2000)

John Bàn MacKenzie,
1796-1864.
From a calotype by D.O. Hill and
R. Adamson. Courtesy of the
Scottish National Portrait Gallery.

Those who babble about its being impossible to play Piobaireachd unless one knows Canntaireachd or have been taught from written Canntaireachd are talking as much rot as those who say you can't play Piobaireachd unless you can talk Gaelic. On a par with saying that you can't eat fish properly unless you can talk Billingsgate*.

Archibald Campbell of Kilberry (1936)

Some Letters of Archibald Campbell of Kilberry 1935-1949, J.H. Shone, editor (The International Piper Ltd.,1980).

Archibald Campbell in 1925 shortly after his appointment as a judge in India

* Billingsgate is the big fish market in London

162

. . . Macqueen walked some miles to give us a convoy. He had joined Prince Charles at Fort Augustus, and continued in the Highland army till after the battle of Culloden. As he narrated the particulars of that unlucky but brave and generous attempt, I several times burst into tears. There is a certain association of ideas in my mind upon that subject, by which I am strongly affected. The very Highland names, or the sound of a bagpipe, will stir my blood and fill me with a mixture of melancholy, and respect for courage; and pity for the unfortunate, and superstitious regard for antiquity; and inclination for war without thought; and, in short, with a crowd of sensations.

James Boswell (1773)

Boswell's Tour to the Hebrides

With the view of studying the class of sounds inaudible to certain ears, we would recommend it to the young naturalist to examine the sounds emitted by the insect tribe, both in relation to their effect upon the human ear, and to the mechanism by which they are produced. The Cicadae or locusts in North America appear, from the observations of Dr Hildreth, to be furnished with a bagpipe on which they play a variety of notes. "When any one passes," says he, "they make a great noise and screaming with their air-bladder or bagpipes. These bags are placed under, or rather behind, the wings in the axilla, something in the manner of using the bagpipes with the bags under the arms – I could compare them to nothing else; and, indeed, I suspect the first inventor of the instrument borrowed his ideas from some insect of this kind."

David Brewster (1834)

from *Lectures on Natural Magic*, by David Brewster
(Edinburgh Journal of Science, 1834)

. . . The games were of the usual sort now common – dancing, piping, lifting a heavy stone, throwing the hammer, and running from the Island to Invergarry and back, six miles. The young men who ran came in exhausted, and almost in a state of nudity, for they had thrown off their kilts on the way, and arrived in their shirts only. A blanket was cast over them and a glass of whisky administered.

One feat which I never saw since was twisting the four legs from a cow, for which a fat sheep was offered as a prize. The cow was brought up and felled before the multitude, and the barbarous competition began, several men making the attempt. At last one man succeeded. After struggling for about an hour, he managed to twist off the four legs, and as a reward received his sheep, with a eulogistic speech from the chief in Gaelic . . .

Joseph Mitchell (c1820)

Reminiscences of My Life in the Highlands
– Mitchell was describing a highland games in Glengarry.
At the 1822 Northern Meeting in Inverness, Colonel
Alasdair Ranaldson MacDonell, 15th of Glengarry,
staged a smiliar spectacle in what he termed
a 'True Highland Games' . . .

It is to catch its echoing tones among the blue mountains of its native country; to sit on the heather banks beside the stilly loch and ancient Dun; listening to the notes so sweetly mellowed by distance, as they swell on the evening breeze: to hear the melody wafted o'er the silent lake, or breaking through the roaring of the mountain-stream and rushing of the fitful wind, – thus it is to hear the Bag-Pipe as it ought to be heard.

James Logan (1838)

A Collection of Ancient Piobaireachd or Highland Pipe Music by Angus MacKay

Dùn Boreraig, Skye

The clansmen on every side stript their plaids, prepared their arms, and there was an awful pause of about three minutes, during which the men, pulling off their bonnets, raised their faces to heaven, and uttered a short prayer; then pulled their bonnets over their brows, and began to move forward at first slowly. Waverley felt his heart at that moment throb as it would have burst from his bosom. It was not fear, it was not ardour, – it was a compound of both, a new and deeply energetic impulse, that with its first emotion chilled and astounded, then fevered and maddened his mind. The sounds around him combined to exalt his enthusiasm; the pipes played, and the clans rushed forward, each in its own dark column. As they advanced they mended their pace, and the muttering sounds of the men to each other began to swell into a wild cry.

Sir Walter Scott (1814)

Waverley

John MacColl . . . lived entirely through teaching piping and competing at Highland games. Nobody in the history of piping had done this before, and nobody has done it since. He was the first truly professional piper since the MacCrimmons.

Seumas MacNeill
(1998)

Piping Times, March 1998

Somerled [Macdonald] was fascinated by the cyclists who hurtled round the track whilst we were trying to concentrate on the piping. He always hoped to see a good crash, and if he saw a possible one building up he would leave his seat at the judges' table and peep round the side of the hut. Admittedly he only did this when some very poor player (and we heard many in those days) was grinding his way through a tune which we had easily damned as 'Below Standard'. Any remonstrances were met by some such remarks as 'I know this fellow – he's hopeless' . . .

Frank Richardson (1987)

Piobaireachd and its Interpretation (John Donald, 1987)
– see Notes on p294

Early the first morning after we arrived on Skye, Sabhal Mor Ostaig lent us a small van, and we drove to Boreraig. We had a little picnic there, and a few players played some piobaireachd at the site, and we read some historic accounts of the MacCrimmons.

People at the school never stopped coming to me and telling me how meaningful that was for them. It put everything together. They had been given information, totally devoid of a feeling for where it came from. Now, they were getting the connection, realising that the piobaireachd was composed in very rough, natural surroundings, not from some luxurious academy of music in a large city.

Donald Lindsay (1999)
– on bringing his summer school to Skye. From *the Voice*, Summer 1999

. . . But Somerled overstepped the forgiveable limit one day when a 'hardy annual' competitor was laboriously pursuing his annual pilgrimage in search of the Holy Grail – the Gold Medal. Somerled related in a loud voice how at Nairn Games a famous film star had seized him and another Highland veteran by their arms and swung them round to face a press photographer. In case we missed the point he left the shelter and demonstrated what had happened, turning his back on the luckless competitor.

Frank Richardson (1987)

Piobaireachd and its Interpretation (John Donald, 1987)
– see Notes on p294

If there's two ways of playing a thing, surely you're allowed to make a preference, or you wouldn't be a musician. We don't want a crowd, like we've nearly got, a crowd of clones walking about. We started with pipers long before we started with sheep!

P/M Angus MacDonald, MBE (1998)

The Voice, Autumn/Fall 1998

Bobs Brown and Nicol
– the 'Bobs of Balmoral'

Them? Teach pipin'? They nivver taught a piper in their lives. They're jist finishers o' pipers, french polishers. Sittin' at the fire croonin' piobaireachd. Tchach!

Bessie Brown (c1970)

– quoted in *The Highland Pipe and Scottish Society 1750-1950* by William Donaldson. Bessie Brown was Bob Brown's sister.

I am sensible that my taste in music must be inelegant and vulgar, because people of undisputed and cultivated taste can find no merit in many of my favourite tunes. Still because I am cheaply pleased, is that any reason why I should deny myself that pleasure? Many of our strathspeys, ancient and modern, give me exquisite enjoyment where you and other judges would probably be showing signs of disgust . . . in fact unless I be pleased with the tune I never can make verses to it.

Robert Burns (1794)

– Burns was addressing music publisher John Thomson complaining about the arrangements of some of his songs by composers such as Pleyel, Haydn and Beethoven. Taken from Dr Fred Freeman's talk to the Lowland & Border Pipers' Society in November 2002 and published in *Common Stock* – the journal of the LBPS – in December 2002

Robert Burns and
Ludwig van Beethoven

. . . At Fort William one of the judges could neither play the pipes nor had he any knowledge of competitions or pipe music whatsoever. To my amazement this 'judge' asked me, while the piper was still tuning up his pipes if he had begun to play his tune! It used to be a rule in the [Piobaireachd] Society's competitions that the piper should not be allowed to tune his pipes on the platform. It has since struck me that perhaps this rule was made in order to enable the judges to guess with tolerable accuracy when the piper actually did commence.

Somerled MacDonald (1910)

Oban Times, April 1910
– taken from *The Highland Pipe and Scottish Society 1750-1950*
by William Donaldson (Tuckwell Press, 2000). See Notes on p294

. . . But I never heard that any of the young lads in Eigg had the luck of MacCrimmon. It was from the Folk of the Bruth [the Fairy-den] that he got his share of music, and little was that same share. Three of them came to him as he lay weeping on the knoll, and said to the first: "I will give thee the championship of piping." Said the second: "I will give thee the championship of goodly company." Said the third: "Two championships are enough for any man; I will put an ill along with them – the madness of the full moon." And as it is the unlikely thing that often happens, better was the ill than the good, for the MacCrimmons never played so well as when the moon was full and the madness lay upon them. Hast ever heard of the two night-wanderers who were passing a wood near Dunvegan Castle? Said the one to the other: "Are they not the two beautiful things, the full moon in the sky and the music of the mavis in yonder wood?" "It is not the mavis at all," said the other; "it is Padruig Mor MacCrimmon, and the warbling of the mavis in his fingers."

Kenneth MacLeod (1927)

The Road to the Isles

Full Moon Above Dunvegan Castle by Stuart Letford

Angus McPherson: "Well, John, who will we give the prizes to?"
John MacDonald, Inverness: "It doesn't matter, Angus: they've killed the piobaireachd, they've killed the piobaireachd!"

Angus MacPherson and John MacDonald (c1930s)

– after judging at a Highland Games in the 1930s.
Quoted by David Murray in *The Piper Press*, No. 7

Ta feedil, pha iss ta feedil to ta piobmhor? Can ta feedil speak to you as ta pipes will, my pretty man, when the ball cartridge will be loose in your pooch and your snider shoe-block is het? And will your feedils or your tam brass bands be able to give you wan plaw when the paignet is on ta snider and it is 'Capper Fay gu pra', or eternal tamnation? No py cot, ta pipes is ta best what effer.

'Old Kenneth' (1877)

Pipers and Pipe Music in a Highland Regiment by I.H. MacKay Scobie

The bagpipes are a useless relic of the barbarous ages and not in any manner calculated to discipline troops!

General Sir Eyre Coote (1778)

– Coote was the Commander-in-Chief of the British forces in India during the 1780s

If John MacKenzie piper of Taymouth knows of any good looking lad, skillful on the Bagpipes, *sober and well educated* I'll make him a Sergeant and Piper Major.

Lauderdale Maule (1847)

Highland Soldier 1820-1920 by Diana M. Henderson
(John Donald, 1989)

There are monks in Tibet who have postcards of Scottish dancers – pre-pubescent girls in mini-skirts and velvet jackets prancing up and down on top of blunt crossed swords. Yet, when you stop to think about what these dancers are actually doing, this most popular of tourist attractions is a parody of everything it is supposed to stand for. The Highlanders were warriors who stamped and crashed their feet in time to the wail of the bagpipes, working themselves into a fighting frenzy and their enemies into a state of terror. When they danced on swords they were the bloody swords of fallen enemies.

Jan-Andrew Henderson (2000)

The Emperor's New Kilt

Far am bi na faigh richean is ann a bhios na pìobairean,
Far am bi na pìobairean is ann a bhios na dannsairean.
Far am bi na dannsairean is ann a bhios na caileagan,
Far am bì na caileagan is dòchagum bi buaireas ann.

Neo-aithnichte
– bho *An Fhaighir Mhuileach*

Where the fairs are the pipers will be,
Where the pipers are the dancers will be,
Where the dancers are the girls will be,
Where the girls are, there turmoil is expected.

Unknown
– from *The Mull Fair*

It is a strange thing that the only monument to a piper in Scotland is situated many miles from the bagpipe lands of the MacCrimmons, the MacKays, the Rankines, the MacArthurs and other cradles of bagpipe tradition. However, considering that Glasgow is today the hub of piping, the situation of Habbie Simpson's monument in Kilbarchan is quite appropriate, as it can be visited on a Glasgow Corporation bus . . . The statue is unique, and discloses that the bagpipe was held in great esteem in lowland Scotland at the same time as the MacCrimmons of Skye were developing their art of Ceol Mor.

Thomas Pearston
(1953)
Piping Times, July 1953

I met Mackay [John], Raasay's piper. The fame of this man is too well known to require any praise from me. He is not satisfied with the treatment he is receiving, and as his abilities are unnoticed and his allowance so reduced that he cannot exist, he talks as a last resource of going to America. To let this man leave the Highlands will bring deserved obloquy on these institutions who have it in their power to relieve one so capable of preserving in purity the strains of our beloved ancestors, and, in the event of his quitting his native land we lose a treasure, as he will leave none behind him worthy of being his successor. I asked him if he would become a teacher of his instrument if he got a situation by which he could live; his reply was that he would do anything rather than leave his country. He thought from £40-£50 per annum would be an ample provision, and will the London, the Edinburgh, the Fort William, the Tain, and the Celtic Societies allow this man to emigrate for such a trifle – for the honour of our country, I hope not.

William MacKenzie (1821)

– see Notes on p294

"He [John MacColl] did tell me of finishing a dance, throwing off his kilt (having running shorts underneath), competing in the hundred yards race and then putting his kilt and things on ready for the next dance. This, of course, was just as a professional to augment his prize money for the day. Naturally his major earnings came from playing the pipes, dancing and teaching.

John Carruthers MacColl (c1955)

– recalling his famous father
Quoted by Seumas MacNeill in *Piping Times*, March 1998

John MacColl (far right) dancing at Tomintoul Highland Games, c1900

When I won my [Gold] Medal in 1947, I called down to visit John [MacDonald, Inverness] during the tea break. "Well MacLeod, I hear you got the medal today!"

"Yes, Mr. MacDonald".

"What did you play?"

"Cille Chriosda"*.

"You just have time to play it over before tea."

There was nothing easier! I'm the Gold Medalist; I can play this tune even before John MacDonald – and I did, finishing with what I considered to be a fine flourish. There was a dearthly hush when I finished, and like some of the famous concert artistes of the past, I waited for my dues. I got them!

"MacLeod," he said, "Did they give you the medal for *that*?"

Pipe-Major Donald MacLeod (1962)

Piping Times, February 1962

* Glengarry's March

Archie MacNeill

I had entered for the piobaireachd competition, and when the judges asked what tune I was going to play I told them 'Seaforth's Salute'. I was then requested to play the ground work and one of the variations as that would be sufficient – not much encouragement for a beginner. However, I played the tune right through from beginning to end. I had paid my entry money and I could not reason why I should carry out their instructions.

Archie MacNeill (1960)

Piping Times, March 1960

Many of his [Peter MacLeod] tunes had a distinctive touch and were unique for his era – for example *The Conundrum*, which has an interesting story and has nothing to do with the way he walked. It was first played by the composer's son Peter R. at a meeting of the Scottish Pipers' Association probably in 1930. One can imagine the mixed reception it had. The name *The Conundrum* was applied to the tune by Peter's eldest sister on hearing it for the first time. It certainly is a very unusual march and only in later years has its similarity to *Glengarry's Lament* been publicly noted.

Angus J. MacLellan (1998)

Piping Times, January 1998

Peter R. MacLeod
1878-1965

. . . The coffin was borne breast high by eighteen Highlanders who relieved each other at regular intervals. The chief mourner was the young chief of Glengarry, (the only surviving son of the late *MacMhic Alasdair,*) dressed in the full Highland garb of his ancestors, with eagle's feathers in his bonnet covered with crape. Some hundreds of the people were arrayed in the Highland garb. The mournful piobaireachd [Glengarry's Lament] was wailed forth by six pipers . . .

Angus MacKay (1838)

Baptism was in the home. Baptism was not held in church at all. But the minister would be going (very often with his family along with him) to the house where an infant was to be baptised, and the baptism would be done in the house, and after the baptism we would have a great feast with a piper playing the pipes and drams going. A happy and pleasant time it was, baptism in the house.

Donald W. MacKenzie (1992)

Island Voices (Birlinn 2002)

As a boy I was taught the bagpipe scale with the open C, which I presume is meant by having the little finger up. Like many others however, I found that to suit the modern chanter it required to keep the little finger on so as to get a sharper and clearer C note, and in this way it became quite popular, but could in no way condemn the former method.

In my earlier instruction no piper would ever dream of making a closed C note and we have definite knowledge that Angus MacKay, to whom we owe so much, taught from his own fingers the open C. I would suggest that, rather than condemn either method, it be left to the discretion of the performer and accept either way as correct. In my judging, and I do quite a lot of it, I act in this manner.

Angus MacPherson (1954)

Piping Times, August 1954

Frequently has the writer listened with delight to the tales of pastoral life led by the people on these occasions, – when free from care, they tended their flocks among the pastures of the upland common.

The men occasionally visited the low grounds to attend their simple husbandry then in use, or to procure some of the delicious fish which abound along the coast; some engaged in the chase, or followed the game; and richly did they deem themselves rewarded for their toil When returning to the family circle, the produce of the flocks and dairy were put before them, and the feast enlivened by the pure essence of mountain dew, joined to the heart-stirring strains of the bagpipe.

Rev. D. McArthur (1843)

New Statistical Account, Ulva entry

Clann Duiligh or Clann Mhic Raing (Rankin) played on MacLean's right flank in battles. They settled at Kilbrennan, and one of them learned his art from the fairies at the Sithein of Lagan Ulva. The fairies gave him *feadan sithe Chloinn Duiligh* (the fairy chanter of Clann Duiligh) and taught him the 'Glas Mheur' (the Finger Lock) – a 'hidden tune'. MacRaing's daughter learned the tune and passed it on to one of her father's pupils who was courting her. When this pupil had completed his training at the piping college at Kilbrennan he had to play all he had learned before MacRaing who was so impressed by his young pupil's performance that he asked him to play more. He played the 'hidden tune' that the daughter had taught him, and when he had finished, MacRaing reached for his sword and went after him.

Neil Rankin Morison (c1934)

Island Voices (Birlinn 2002)

The piobaireachd man is ominous and tragic, and the heavy stare of his large and motionless eyes conveys the impression of dreary contempt and smouldering passion; and the far-off look of tragedy in his set and melancholy gaze is so often veiled in impenetrable concentration. His instrument and he, when they become One, have their stamping ground on the gore of battlefield, at the graveside when "tears trickle down the granite walls," or, as is more usual, in the late hours, while most mortals are horizontal and dormant, when he can hypnotise large tracts of the human mind, and then imbed in the brains of his audience what was implied rather than what he played.

Dr Roderick Ross (1959)

Binneas Is Boreraig (College of Piping, 1959)

(Piobaireachd Dhunnaomhaig)

As soon as Coll's [Colla *Ciotach* MacDonald, a Gaelic hero] advance party arrived at the castle [Dunyveg, Islay] they were made prisoners. Next day, Coll furtively left his secret lair and sailed away for Dunyveg, and when his galley was seen sailing directly for the castle the conspirators were delighted. Their deadly foeman was sailing right into the muzzles of the guns of the stronghold. In order to allay any suspicion Coll might have regarding their good intentions they conceived the idea of releasing the piper, so that Coll might see and hear him playing the pipes on the battlements, and thus get the impression that all was well. Little did they know that Coll and his piper had perfected a system whereby the piper, by means of his chanter, could warn his master of danger. As soon as the piper saw his beloved master almost within the jaws of the trap, he struck up and played the celebrated *Piper's Warning to his Master* . . . As soon as Coll heard the warning notes of Mac-an-Riabhach's chanter, he at once put about and sailed away. The plotters were extremely chagrined when their quarry escaped them. The sudden manner in which Coll had turned away could only allow of one explanation. Suspicion fell on the piper and he was cruelly tortured.

Duncan Johnston, Islay

– date unknown. *Colkitto! A Celebration of Clan Donald of Colonsay (1570-1647)* by Kevin Byrne (House of Lochar, 1997)

with his reward (which was great in this country, being no less than one pound four shillings), he expressed his gratitude by playing a voluntary on his pipe for more than half an hour, as he strided backward and forward outside the house under our window.

Here is gentility in disguise; and I am sorry to say that this kind of vanity in people of no fortune makes them ridiculous to strangers, and I wish they could divest themselves of it, and apply to something more substantial than the airy notion of 'ancient family', which, by extending our thoughts, we shall find may be claimed by all of mankind.

Edmund Burt (1754)

Letters from a Gentleman in the North of Scotland

. . . One must also keep in mind that many features once common throughout pre-industrial Europe survived longest in the 'Celtic Fringe' and are now mistakenly thought of as being specifically 'Celtic', such as bagpipes, step-dancing, fiddle music, keening, wakes, pre-Christian nature celebrations, and so on. We must be careful to use the term Celtic in ways which are accurate and meaningful.

Michael Newton (2000)

A Handbook of the Scottish Gaelic World
(Four Courts Press, 2000)

Did the Bretons borrow the bagpipe OR the idea of the pipe band (called the *bagad*, which, basically, is a pipe band with added *bombardes*)? . . . Paradoxically, the success of the *biniou bras* [in Brittany] ensured the survival of the *biniou koz*, which found a new public and new performers. The latter requiring no particular training for an experienced bagpiper, many were prepared to have a go at it and adopt it whenever they wanted to return to the roots of Breton music.

Jean-Francois Allain (1995)

Piping Times, February 1995

* The biniou bras – the Great Highland Bagpipe – was introduced to Brittany after the Second World War; the biniou koz is the traditional Breton bagpipe.

From *Bagpipe Music*

Let me play to you tunes without measure or end,
Tunes that are born to die without a herald,
As a flight of storks rises from a marsh, circles,
And alights on the spot from which it rose.

Flowers. A flower-bed like hearing the bagpipes.
The fine black earth has clotted into sharp masses
As if the frost and not the sun had come.
First faint rose peonies, then peonies blushing,
The again red peonies, and behind them,
Massive, apoplectic peonies, some of which are so red
And so violent as to seem almost black; behind these
Stands a low hedge of larkspur, whose tender apologetic blossoms

Appear by contrast pale, though some, vivid as the sky above them,
Stand out from their fellows, iridescent and slaty as a pigeon's
    breast.
The bagpipes – they are screaming and they are sorrowful.
There is a wail in their merriment, and cruelty in their triumph.
They rise and they fall like a weight swung in the air at the end of a
    string.
They are like the red blood of those peonies.
And like the melancholy of those blue flowers.
They are like human voice – no! for the human voice lies!
They are like human life that flows under the words.
That flower-bed is like the true life that wants to express itself
And does . . . while we human beings lie cramped and fearful.

Hugh MacDiarmid (1943)

. . . the style of Highland instrumental music is based on the song tradition, for, as can be found in all folk cultures, instrumentalists were in the habit of playing tunes that they and their audience were already familiar with as songs.

This is particularly evident in the fact that the bagpiper took the place of singers when occasion called for it, and he must have taken the appropriate repertoire of songs into his collection of tunes. Parties of reapers are sometimes described as working to the sound of the pipes, and their is no reason to doubt that he would have played the tunes of their reaping songs. When the practice of keening was effectively banned, the bagpiper led the procession and often seems to have adopted the music of the keening songs.

Michael Newton (2000)

A Handbook of the Scottish Gaelic World by Michael Newton
(Four Courts Press, 2000)

The highlight of the competition [1998 Argyllshire Gathering] for me was *The Red Speckled Bull*. There were two of them. One had been especially prepared for the show ring. Its hair had been brushed until the coat glistened. The hooves and horns had been burnished. It walked with a stately grace and a superior look.

This was Dr Angus MacDonald's creation. The other, Allan MacDonald's beast, had a wicked glint in its eye. It pawed the ground; steam emanated from flared nostrils. Its matted hair was festooned with dried excrement. For excitement this was the *Bull* for me.

Ian K. Murray (1998)

– at the Argyllshire Gathering that year.
From the *Piping Times*, October 1998

I am not inclined to question the age or the genuineness of the Celtic civilisation, for the Highlanders have all the marks of a highly civilised people. But in Scotland that civilisation has always been disunited for one thing, and for another has left behind it an astonishing meagre record of its existence. A little poetry, a number of lovely songs, some beautiful pipe music, hardly any sculpture or architecture, no painting, no philosophy, no science, and so sign of that conceptual intelligence which welds together and creates great and complex communities and makes possible the major achievements of art and science.

Edwin Muir (1935)

Scottish Journey

Contrary to popular belief, the bagpipes have suffered not from any act prohibiting their use after Culloden – no such act ever existed – but from the lack of native institutions. The British military became the principal patron of bagpiping and competitions in the Lowlands and at Highland Games were the new means of achieving prestige in the piping world. As the contests were far removed from the Gaelic world, they enabled the introduction of ideas and styles once foreign to Gaelic music. Improvers made bagpiping a 'literate art' (in contrast to previous oral and aural styles of teaching), regularised tunes according to written notation and Western art music ideas of musicality (levelling out the Gaelic idiom), and changed the tempo.

Michael Newton (2000)

A Handbook of the Scottish Gaelic World by Michael Newton
(Four Courts Press, 2000)

It is the custom for the piper who pulls off the major prizes to pipe for dancing. On this occasion when the dancers were called, the piper appeared in a blue suit and bowler hat. The judge, astonished, called him over and enquired what this rig-out meant. And the piper explained that as he wanted to catch an early train he thought he would save time by changing his clothes before he started piping for the dancing. He had collected all the money in quick time and now he wanted to 'beat it' at the earliest moment in the bowler hat of decency . . . The judge, however, thought otherwise and in lucid terms returned the hero to his tent.

Neil M. Gunn (1931)

The Man Who Came Back

The time has gone as far as I am concerned for being judged by people who are sitting and looking at gracenotes. Expecting you to decorate a tune exactly as it is written in a script is a lot of nonsense.

Allan MacDonald (2004)
Piping World, May 2004 (Duntroon Publishing)

This man [Gordon Duncan] is precious and should be one of Scotland's living national treasures.

Hamish Moore (1994)
– in the sleevenotes to Gordon's CD
Just for Seumas

Malcolm MacPherson c1890s

If your son cannot learn without the paper you should keep him at home.

Malcolm MacPherson (c1890)

Oban Times, July 1940
– taken from Robert Meldrum's 'Reminiscences'
where he recalled sending his son to
MacPherson for lessons with tunes written
down on paper.

210

. . . In the fighting during the pursuit of the French forces north and through the Pyrenees in 1813, the 92nd made a desperate bayonet charge at Maya. There was fierce fighting for the Gordons on the Nivelle, and in the advance to Bayonne. At St. Pierre their pipers played to the death. When one fell, another took up the air, and when he went down a third continued it.

William Pratt Paul (1969)

History of the Scottish Regiments

Kenneth MacKay at Waterloo

We're always there if a few pounds are going,
Blowing like hell – nothing but blowing,
Doing our best old memories back to bring,
By piping, sword dance, reel and the fling.

David C. Mather (1899)
– quoted by Bridget MacKenzie in *Piping Traditions of the North of Scotland* (John Donald 1998)

Having become a pupil of John MacDonald during my sick leave, I was later able for more than a year, whilst stationed at Fort George, to go to him for lessons nearly every Saturday. So far as I can remember I paid for a lesson from 2 to 3pm; but John's sister, Mrs Anderson, having given us a cup of tea around 5pm, would ask at about 7pm if we were never going to be finished. Sometimes there would be still more piping after supper; and at last I would drive home to the Fort, so intoxicated (on tea and ceol mor) that I once drove into a ditch, still chanting the tunes we had discussed.

Frank Richardson (1987)

Piobaireachd and its Interpretation
(John Donald Publishers Ltd., 1987)

General Richardson

We had a bold tune from the piper, a decent comely fellow with a green cloth waistcoat with silver lace; and then he helped to serve at table. His name was Neill Rankin. These Rankins have been pipers to the family of Maclean for many generations. They used to have a college in Mull for teaching the bagpipe, but it has not been in practice now for sixteen years . . .

James Boswell (1773)

Boswell's Tour to the Hebrides

If you get involved too much, and start thinking about piobaireachd too much, you could end up going off your head!

Willie Ross (c1950)
– quoted by John D. Burgess
Piper & Drummer magazine, February 1995

215

. . . O! that I had been at more pains, to gather those admirable remains of our ancient Highland music, before I left my native country. It would have augmented my collection of Highland music and poetry, which I have formed a system of, in my voyage to India, and propose to send soon home, dedicated to Sir James McDonald, or some such chieftain of rank and figure in the Highlands, in order that those sweet, noble, and expressive sentiments of nature, may not be allowed to sink and die away: and to shew, that our poor remote corner, even without the advantages of learning and cultivation, abounded in works of taste and genius . . . My good friend Mr M. at London, has been so kind as to send me a fine Highland bagpipe, and a suit of Highland cloaths, which, I hear, have arrived at a town on the coast of Malabar, with which I expect yet to make a conquest of an Indian princess.

Joseph MacDonald (1760)

– quoted by his brother, Patrick, in his *Collection of Highland Vocal Airs* (1784)

I have hard the story that MacCrimmon would write down a tune on the wet sand as the tide began to ebb, and would expect his pupils to be able to play it before the flood tide once more flowed over the sand and washed away the marks.

Seton Gordon (1947)

A Highland Year

Looking west from Dun Boreraig, Skye

The Piper o' Perth

The piper o' Perth was a laddie o' smeddum,
O' braw strappin' callans that toon has nae dearth;
An' mony a lassie would blythly hae wed him,
But, "Deil tak' them a'," said the piper o' Perth.

"I lo'e but ae sweethe'rt, an' her I lo'e blindly,
The bag in my oxter's the mistress for me;
I cuddle her closely, an' oh! but she's kindly,
She aye has a sang for my dule or my glee.

The North Inch, Perth

"The pipes are my dawtie, the pipes are my dearie,
I tread the North Inch like a lord o' the earth,
An' back frae Kinnoull comes the echo sae cheerie,
When wooin' his love gaes the piper o' Perth.

"An' leal is my he'rt, for I'm nae gallivanter,
The pipes mak' me fain like nae lassie on earth."
But, shame tak' the vaunter; his drone an' his chanter
He's laid at the feet o' a fair maid o' Perth.

W. D. Cocker (1932)

Poems, Scots and English

---

smeddum – spirit; *strappin'* – tall and strong; *callans* – boys; *oxter* – under the arm;
dule – sorrow; *dawtie* – darling; *Kinnoull* – the hill above Perth; *leal* – loyal;
gallivanter – philanderer; *fain* – eager, desirous;

At the Cowal Games, Dunoon

Haveran, bletheran, yatteran folk
thrang the streets roun the pier,
ilka Jeannie lays haud o her Jock
an bangs her wey thru the steer.

There's tartan tammies an muckle blads
tae shaw the garb o the clans:
there's thisl't lassies an kiltit lads
wi the emblems o fitba fans.

The whussle an jostle an rankringan din,
the stour an the heat o the day
are suddentlie naethin, for aa are kin
whan the thoosand pipers play.

As the skirlan soun drifts up tae the hills
an spreids owre the skinklan sea,
there's fient a breist but gaes faster and fills
wi whit Scotland yince could be.

Yet afore the echo has cool't i the bluid,
there's blawan o gee-gaws again,
an Scotland's back tae her doited mood
o snichteran, sneet, hauf-men!

Maurice Lindsay

– date unknown. *Collected Poems 1940-1990*

Haveran, bletheran, yatteran – over-wordy; *bangs* – pushes; *steer* – crowd;
muckle blads – posters; *fient a breist* – not one

Playing the bagpipes within doors is a Lowland and English custom. In the Highlands the piper is always in the open air, and when people wish to dance to the music, it is on the open grass if the weather permits; nothing but necessity makes them attempt a pipe dance in the house.

Major-General David Stewart of Garth (1822)

Sketches of . . . the Highlanders of Scotland

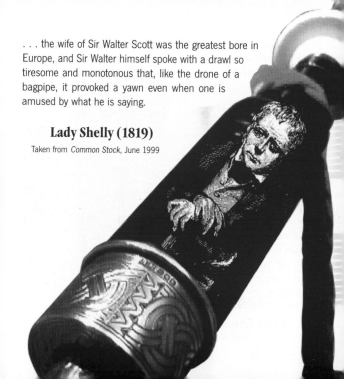

. . . the wife of Sir Walter Scott was the greatest bore in Europe, and Sir Walter himself spoke with a drawl so tiresome and monotonous that, like the drone of a bagpipe, it provoked a yawn even when one is amused by what he is saying.

Lady Shelly (1819)

Taken from *Common Stock*, June 1999

Calum [MacPherson] was easily the best player of piobaireachd I have ever known. He hardly ever played march, strathspey and reel, only piobaireachd and jigs. Each morning Calum used to play jigs on the chanter while breakfast was being got ready – he used to sit near the peat fire as he played . . . I can see him now, with his old jacket and his leather sporran, sitting on a stool while the porridge was being brought to the boil. After breakfast he would take his barrow to the peat moss, cut a turf, and build up the fire with wet peat for the day. He would then sit down beside me, take away all books and pipe music, then sing in his own canntaireachd the ground and different variations of the particular piobaireachd he wished me to learn.

John MacDonald, Inverness (1942)

– recalling Malcolm MacPherson (Calum Piobaire) in the *Oban Times*, April 1942.

Calum Piobaire's
old house in Badenoch

Many a story did old John [Bàn] MacKenzie tell me when I was turning his lathe for him and learning music with him. He was four score when he died and that is more than twenty years ago. It must be nearly a hundred years since he was in Raasay, learning 'Ceòl mòr', great music, from [John] Mackay . . . they only played Ceòl mòr on the pipes, battle tunes, and laments, and salutes, and such like. They had cattle in one end of their house. Mackay used to turn his back to the pupils, and play the tunes. Mackay's sister used to sit by the fire, and dictate the words of Canntaireachd and sing them as the piper played.

Duncan Ross (c1860)

Taken from *The Highland Pipe and Scottish Society, 1750-1950*, by William Donaldson
(Tuckwell Press, 2000)

Sir, – Can you or any of the numerous readers of the *Oban Times* inform me how it is that Piobaireachd is the only species of the music of the Gael that has neither time, tune, melody, nor rhythm in it? Did the composers intend to puzzle and annoy, or is it the performers who vie with each other in prolonging unconnected, meaningless sounds? I have recently listened to a champion playing what he called the *Massacre of Glencoe*, but really no one could make head or tail of it, and [I] am at a loss to understand how an intelligent being could call it a musical performance. I am, &c..

'Celt' (1893)

Oban Times, 1893
Taken from *The Highland Pipe and Scottish Society, 1750-1950*,
by William Donaldson (Tuckwell Press, 2000)

There is in Largs a weekly market on Thursdays, and four annual fairs, the most remarkable of which is St Columba's day, vulgarly called *Comb's day*, which is held on the second Tuesday of June.

This fair is famous over the west of Scotland, and continues from Monday to Thursday. Great numbers of people, from 40 or 50 miles round, resort to it, some for business, and some for pleasure. Upwards of 100 boats are often to be seen, on this occasion, riding in the Bay.

The whole week is a kind of jubilee to the inhabitants, and scene of diversion to others.

Such a vast multitude cannot be accommodated with beds; and the Highlanders, in particular, do not seem to think such accommodation necessary. They spend the whole night in rustic sports, carousing and dancing on the green to the sound of the bagpipe. Every one who chooses is allowed to join in this, which forms their principal amusement. The candidates for the dance are generally so numerous, that it is kept up without intermission during the whole time of the fair.

Unknown (c1799)

The Old Statistical Account, Largs entry

. . . About an hour before day, an expres arrives from Invernesse to inform us yt all the troops were parted about eleven or twelve o'Clock, wt Louden & MccCloud at their head; the Alarm was given imediatly to the Prince, who stript this night contreray to his custom. About half an hour after an other expresse arrives & assures he left Louden about a half mil from the river Nairn, &yt they wou'd infallably be about the house before day. No woman in the world cou'd be in the condition yt poor Lady MccIntosh was in, running about like a mad woman in her shift; every man she saw she took him for the enemy, expresses were sent to all the quarters where our men were, to assemble them in all dilligence; the Prince wth those yt were lodged in the house retired to the wood above the Loc, some of our own troops yt were arriving, were taken for the enemy, so yt every man made the best of his way. About two hours of the day the Smith arrives who cleared up all matters, & brings a sure acct of Loudens being returned to Invernesse. It's most certain yt Louden was in march, & very near the river of Nairn, with a design to surprise the Prince. The Smith who heard them coming, set himself & his ten men out of the road, until he'd be sure it was the enemy; finding it was, he dispers'd his men two by two at a good distance one from another with orders as soon as they wou'd hear them speak, & see his fire, to fire at the same time, & to call, one upon the MccDonalds, another on the Camerons, &ca, yt the enemy may imagine yt all the clans were there. This Scheme succeeded as he cou'd desire; when they were very near to him, he crys out calling upon the Clans in his language, "here they are we have got the Villans at last," & fired, his men did the same, & continued. Loudens detachment did not fire one shot, but dispers'd in a minuit & went of as fast as they cou'd drive, & arrived at Invernesse in the greatest disorder imaginable; MccCloud had his Piper killed just by his side, & was very much laughed at when he came back. The Prince gave the smith some Guineas; he called for a Captns Comission wch the Prince granted him, & really he deserved it, for the most experienc'd partizan cou'd not act better.

John William O'Sullivan (c1747)

– the death of Donald Bàn MacCrimmon. O'Sullivan was one of the 'Seven Men of Moidart' who landed with Prince Charles at Moidart on 25th July, 1745.

– see Notes on p292

. . . In the position of things in the west [the imminent raising of the Standard at Glenfinnan], it was determined by those in authority to reinforce the garrison of Fort William by the two companies of the Royal Scots, drawn from Fort Augustus.

In their journey the soldiers had necessarily to pass through the most disaffected district in Scotland, but nothing unusual occurred till the little party had reached High Bridge, eight miles from Fort William, where they were confronted by a small body of armed Highlanders under Mac Donald of Tirnadrish, who had been hurried forward by Keppoch with a view to, at least, hindering the march while he endeavoured to gather more of his clan together.

Mac Donald, to make the best of the small number of men (eleven and a piper), had placed them behind the Inn to waite for the approach of the enemy, and as soon as they appeared upon the opposite bank above the Bridge he ordered his Piper to play, and rushed out from behind the house with a loud huzza.

By this sudden and unexpected attack ye troops were struck with such an unaccountable panick as with one consent to run of without so much as taking time to observe the number or quality of their enemy, tho to do Captain Scott justice, he endeavoured all in his power to prevail with them to return, but as his brother officers did not show the same spirit or inclination to curiosity his entreaties were of no effect.

Dugald Mitchell (1900)

A Popular History of the Highlands and Gaelic Scotland,

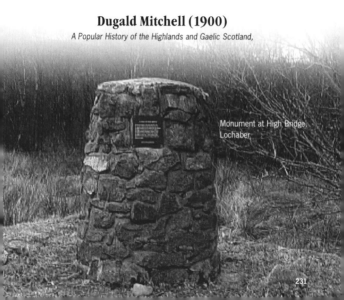

Monument at High Bridge, Lochaber

This mode of dressing the Pipers is no innovation* but that ever since the Regiment was raised they have been this equipt . . . there were always at least two or three Pipers equipped in the old kilted dress of the Regiment who played at its head . . . I may mention that one of the Pipers now in the Regiment has worn the kilt for upwards of seventeen years and another for upwards of twelve years . . . The professional pride of the Pipers themselves (who are not easily procured) would be wounded by the change.

Lt. Colonel Fordyce (1849)

Highland Soldier 1820-1920 by Diana M. Henderson (John Donald, 1989).

---

* "With regard to the innovation introduced into the 74th Regiment of dressing the Pipers in the Kilt. The Commander in Chief orders its immediate discontinuance, and that the Pipers may wear the dress of the Regiment." Adjutant General.

. . . The scene changes to the storming of Badajos, in April, 1812, with the 71st and 74th again heavily engaged. One of the first to mount the castle wall was John McLaughlin, a piper of the 71st. Through the rattle of musketry and crash of cannon could be heard the stirring strains of the ancient Campbell air I've Been To A Wedding In Inveraray as Piper McLaughlin led the assault along the ramparts.

A bullet entered the bag of his pipes and the music stopped. Piper McLaughlin then seated himself on a gun-carriage and busied himself mending the damage, regardless of the shot flying all around him. Soon he again struck up his inspiring battle music.

Later, at the Battle of Vittoria, Piper McLaughlin had both legs shot away by a cannon ball while he was playing beside the Colours. At his request his pipes were handed to him and he continued to play until he died.

William Pratt Paul (1969)

History of the Scottish Regiments

Blast upon blast they blew,
Each clad in tartan new,
Bonnet and blackcock feather:
And every Piper was fou' –
Twenty Pipers together!

Robert Buchanan

– from the 19th century poem *The Wedding of Shon Maclean*

He filled the bag at a breath and swung a lover's arm round about it.
To those who know not the pipes, the feel of the bag in the oxter is a
gaiety lost. The sweet round curve is like a girl's waist; it is friendly and
warm in the crook of the elbow and against a man's side, and to press
it is to bring laughing or tears.

Neil Munro (1896)

The Lost Pibroch

. . . The rain went off. Mist hung about the trees in still air and blanketed the hills. Pipe Major Robert U. Brown walked into the clearing, tuned his pipes, and began to play 'Lament for the Children'. It seemed all other sounds had topped. Could the blackies and the doos be listening too, as the music left the piper, and lifted itself into the hills. No other music could pay such respect to the nativity of the land as it made the past present nor record with such sadness the originating event.

For a time nothing was said until I asked the piper:

"How long does it take to learn to play a pibroch?"

He answered: "It takes seven years to learn to play the pipes, and seven years to learn to play a pibroch, and then you need the poetry."

George Bruce (c1972)

– radio interview with P/M Brown

From *My Heart is like Oceans*

No sound of organ or fiddle,
No flowing music of pipes and of strings,
Nothing played in an otherworld palace
Was ever sweeter than the pipes in your frame:
Breath like the herbs of the moorland
Comes out of your mouth's gentle windows,
The warm-worded, beautiful lips
Of the girl of most ivory-white teeth.

Zachary MacAulay (c1700)

– see Notes on p294

How often have I felt proud of my regiment and comrades while wheeling with the pipes to take up the position of the Salute to play the companies in column past the C.O. There to witness the seasoned soldier with sturdy limbs, bonnet cocked to the side, the kilt giving the proper swing, the rifle at the slope, and from the ranks often a cheery nod or friendly wave, saying as much, "that's the stuff, carry on." But what has been the reward of the piper? None but that which I think cannot better be summed up in the words of a very gallant Highland soldier, the late Colonel Malcolm MacNeill of Colonsay, and these were, "I would rather be Pipe Major than Colonel any day."

Pipe Major William Gray (c1950)

– from his handwritten notes, which were without title or date but appear to be for a lecture to the Scottish Pipers Association. See Notes on p292

From *Lament for the Great Music*

My duty done, I will try to follow you on the last day of the world,
And pray I may see you all standing shoulder to shoulder
With Patrick Mòr MacCrimmon and Duncan Bàn MacCrimmon in the centre
In the hollow at Boreraig or in front of Dunvegan Castle
Or on the lip of the broken graves in Kilmuir Kirkyard,
While, the living stricken ghastly in the eternal light
And the rest of the dead all risen blue-faced from their graves
(Though, the pipes to your hand, you will be once more
Perfectly at ease, and as you were in your prime)
All ever born crowd the islands and the West Coast of Scotland
Which has standing room for them all, and the air curdled with angels,
And everywhere that feeling seldom felt on the earth before

Save in the hearts of parents or in youth untouched by tragedy
That in its very search for personal experience often found
A like impersonality and self-forgetfulness,
And you playing: 'Farewell to Scotland, and the rest of the earth,'
The only fit music there can be for that day
– And I will leap then and hide behind one of you,
A's caismeachd phìob-mòra bras-shròiceadh am puirt. *

Look! Is that only the setting sun again?
Or a piper coming from far away?

Hugh MacDiarmid (1956)

* 'While the notes of the great pipes shrilly sound out their cries'
    (from Alasdair Mac Mhaighstir Alasdair).

The general supposition concerning the modern Highland Bagpipe is that it is superior in tonal quality to that of the bagpipe used in the Highlands during the middle of the sixteenth century (when piping was at its apex) or prior to that time, but is this supposition correct?

If such exponents as the MacCrimmons, MacArthurs and others of note played upon pipes inferior in tonal quality to the average bagpipe, I cannot see how these old masters got a great deal of satisfaction in trying to please their audiences.

Judging by the standard which a trained ear would demand, the inference is that the pipes of the 'Old Boys' was equally good in tonal quality as those of present day manufacture, perhaps better.

Their pibrochs demanded faultless notes from fautless chanters otherwise these would have been little playing as well as speedy decadence in the art.

Pipe Major William Gray (1939)

Piping and Dancing, vol. 5, no. 3

Each day at eight Carnegie was awakened by his piper, a morning harbinger who started his notes at a distance, gradually approaching the castle, which he circled, pausing and skirling beneath the windows of the guests. All went to breakfast to the tones of the organ, which discoursed also throughout the meal. "My morning devotions", Carnegie called this music.

Burton J. Hendrick (1933)

The Life of Andrew Carnegie

Andrew
Carnegie

. . . he observed several people running towards the river of Lochy, and throwing away their plaids as they run, which he at last came to understand from one he mett by the road was owing to an alarum being given that some of the people who belonged to Cappoch* had attacked two companys of Gn. Sinclair's Regiment upon their march from Fort Augustus to Fort William.

These two companies had been quartered att Perth, and were ordered by Gn. Cope to reinforce the garrison at Fort William, but Cappoch . . . sent Mcdonald of Tirrendrish, a near relation of is own, with eleven men and a Piper to a little Inn at Highbridge to waite their coming till he should gett some of his Clan together.

"Mr Mcdonald, to make the best of a small number of men, had placed them behind the Inn to wait for the approach of the enemy, and as soon as they appeared upon the opposite bank above the Bridge he ordered his Piper to play, and rushed out from behind the house with a loud huzza.

"By this sudden and unexpected attack ye troops were struck with such an unaccountable panick as with one consent to run of without as much as taking time to observe the number or quality of the enemy. They continued to retreat or more properly to run, for about five or six miles.

John Murray of Broughton (1745)

– Secretary to, and friend of, Prince Charles Edward Stuart. See Notes on p295

After much plundering in Brae Ross under Allan Macranald of Lundie, the MacDonalds proceeded to the church of Kilchrist, in which the MacKenzies were at the time worshipping. Surrounding the building they at once set it on fire, and burned to death the whole congregation, the piper the while marching round the building, and drowning the cries of the victims in the shrill notes of that pibroch* which, under its name of Kilchrist, has been employed ever since as the clan tune of the Clanranald of Glengarry.

Dugald Mitchell (1900)

History of the Highlands and Gaelic Scotland

– this atrocity, committed in 1603, was the worst one in a series of raids and ambushes in the long MacDonald-MacKenzie feud. The MacKenzies, in pursuit of the escaping MacDonalds, cornered 37 of them in an inn at Torbreck (OS 26, 648409), near Inverness, and burned them with the house. But Allan escaped, by leaping the chasm of Alltsaigh by Loch Ness and swimming across the loch until he was picked up by his ally Fraser of Foyers.

* Glengarry's March

It was 1979. They weren't ready for us. It would have torn apart the local scene completely if we had won the World Championship. I listen to the recording of that contest every once in a while, and probably the bands are cleaner chanter-wise, but listen to the drones. Nobody puts out a drone sound today like we had then.

James Troy (1995)

Piper and Drummer May 1995

– Troy formed the City of Victoria Pipe Band in 1972. At the World Pipe Band Championships in 1979 the band were placed sixth when many felt it should have been first. The band are often referred to as the best band never to win the World Pipe Band Championship.

It was a delightful evening – still, breathless, clear – as we swept across the broad breast of Loch Maree; and the red light of the sinking sun fell on many a sweet wild recess, amid the labyrinth of islands purple with heath, and overhung by the birch and mountain-ash; or slanted along the broken glades of the ancient forest; or lighted up into a blush the pale stony faces of the tall pyramidal hills. A boat bearing a wedding party was crossing the lake to the white house on the opposite side, and a piper stationed in the bows, was discoursing sweet music that, softened by distance, and caught up by the echoes of the rocks, resembled no strain I had ever heard from the bagpipe before. Even the boatmen rested on their oars, and I had just enough of Gaelic to know that they were remarking how very beautiful it was.

"I wish", said my comrade, "you understood these men: they have a great many curious stories about the loch, that I am sure you would like. See you that large island? It is Island-Maree. There is, they tell me, an old burying-ground on it, in which the Danes used to bury long ages ago, and whose ancient tombstones no man can read. And yon other island beside it is famous as the place on which the good people meet every year to make submission to their queen. There is, they say, a little loch in the island, and another little island in the loch; and it is under a tree on that inner island that the queen sits and gathers kain for the Evil One. They tell me that, for certain, the fairies have not left this part of the country yet.".

Hugh Miller (c1835)

My Schools and Schoolmasters

. . . At that time, in 1926, piobaireachd and piping in general were being so firmly stamped upon in Skye that I was referred to in the pulpit as a young man from Edinburgh come to teach their children the ways of the devil, though I had come to try and learn something about piobaireachd – and found there was nothing to be learned, whereas in the adjacent Catholic island, of course, of South Uist, piobaireachd was being just as actively encouraged. I could tell some, almost unbelievable, stories of the extent to which the church worked evil in Skye.

Now Rothiemurchas* told me that he was once in Dunvegan Castle – I don't know when, what year, I am afraid (you know the way you hear these things and you don't make a note at once) – and he was I think with Seton Gordon. They saw in a glass-fronted cabinet a pile of old manuscript which was written all over in an old script and which appeared to them to be unquestionably the MacCrimmon canntaireachd.

Now he didn't like (even though he was Sheriff of Inverness), he didn't like to break open the cupboard – which was a pity. MacLeod was not in residence – he was in London at the time – and when they got the key and got around to finding out (they had talked a little, they had mentioned their intention to get hold of this thing), when they came back some months later it had gone. And nobody will ever convince Rothiemurchas that it was not the minister who had whipped it.

General Frank Richardson (1974)

Proceedings of the Piobaireachd Society Conference, 1974 (The Piobaireachd Society)
* Sherriff John Grant of Rothiemurchas

Blue Song

I am sad since a week ago
Left on this island, without grass, without shelter.
If I could I'd get back home,
Making the journey
Rightaway to Ullinish of white-hoofed cattle.
Where I grew up,
A little girl breast-fed there by soft-palmed women,
In the house of brown-haired Flora, Lachlan's daughter,
Milkmaid among the cows
Of Roderick Mor MacLeod of the banners.
I have been happy in his great house,
Living it up on the dancefloor,
Fiddle-music making me sleepy,
Pibroch my dawn chorus.
Say hello for me to Dunvegan.

Mary MacLeod (c1670)

– see Notes on p295

. . . Some of us got to the top of a hill, and here we see this Scottish brigade coming right past us going to relieve the infantry. We'd been waiting for replacements but none ever came. These Scots, their uniforms were all ironed and pressed and neat and they were marching in time to the bagpipes. It just tore us all up just to see those guys marching. I don't know why. We were so isolated out there. Nobody cared about us but our families. Those bagpipes made you remember that there was civilisation.

Sgt. Gerald Boudreaux (2003)

Taken from *The Times-Picayune*, Louisiana, USA, and quoted in the
Piping Times, October 2003

Memorandum for Seaforths Piper:–

"Lang may ye live ta play these Tunes wi' glee,
And when ye'll Blaw, ye'll sometimes think of me:

Aonghas MacAoidh"

Angus MacKay (c1854)

– while in Bedlam Hospital, MacKay wrote these words in a manuscript of tunes and sent it to his old friend Donald Cameron. The manuscript is now known as the Seaforth MS.

From *The MacCrimmon Legend – The Madness of Angus MacKay*
by Alistair Campsie (Canongate, 1980)

FRIDAY 3 SEPTEMBER. The day was very wet. Sir Alexander's* piper plays below stairs both at breakfast and dinner, which is the only circumstance of a chief to be found about him.

James Boswell (1773)

Boswell's Tour to the Hebrides
* Sir Alexander MacDonald of Sleat, chief of Clan Donald.

Why are there two side holes on a pipe chanter? These are properly the 'G' note holes, although not fingered. The term sound-holes applied here is incorrect.

Pipe Major William Gray (1939)

Piping and Dancing, vol. 4, no. 7

Then Piper Gunn spoke to the people. *Dolts and draggards and daft loons and gutless as gutted herring you are,* he calls out in his voice like the voice of the wind from the north isles. *Why do you sit on these rocks, weeping?* says he. *For there is a ship coming, says he, on the wings of the morning, and I have heard tell of it, and we must gather our pots and kettles and our shawls and our young ones, and go with it into a new world across the waters . . .* Then Piper Gunn changed his music, and he played the battle music there on the rocks . . . Then what happened? What happened then, to all of them people there homeless on the rocks? They rose and followed! Yes, they rose, then, and they followed, for Piper Gunn's music could put the heart into them and they would have followed him all the way to hell or to heaven with the sound of the pipes in their ears.

Margaret Laurence (1974)
The Diviners

Petrus [Bruno] is credited with having invented sheantaireachd or the 'piper's language,' which he derived from the Bible; and it is further stated that it was a code by which original copies of the Scriptures were preserved from interference and alteration, the key being in Genesis 111. 24: 'So he drove out the man; and he placed at the east of the garden of Eden Cherubims, and a flaming sword which turned every way, to keep the way of the tree of life'. One of the important vocables is 'tre' in various forms. It is said that one method of interpretation of the MacCrimmon music has been handed down by chance through the illness of Mr. Simon Fraser, who became gravely ill as a baby in July, 1853 and at the crisis his mother 'three up her hands and wailed the Lament for the Children in the vocables'. From that moment he began to recover, and Mrs. Fraser afterwards explained the strange singing to him on condition that the would not divulge it for fifty years . . .

George C. B Poulter (1936)

The MacCrimmon Family Origin (Camberley, 1936). See Notes on p292

From *Good-bye Twilight*

Back to the great music, Scottish Gaels. Too long
You have wallowed as in the music of Delius.
Make a heroic effort now to swing yourselves round
To the opposite pole – the genius of Sibelius.
(Out of the West Highlands and Islands of Scotland now
What a symphony should come, more ghastly and appalling
Than Sibelius's gaunt El-Greco-emaciated ecstatic Fourth!
Far beyond *Squinting Peter's Flame of Wrath*
Or *Too Long in This Condition*
But like the great jigs, whirling electrons of musical energy,
Like *The Shaggy Grey Buck* or *The Baldooser*,
Fantastic, incredible, all but impossible to human fingers.)

. . . Out from your melancholy moping, your impotence, Gaels,
(You stir the heart, you think? . . . but surely
One of the heart's main functions is to supply the brain!)
Back into the real world again – the world of *The Barren Rocks of Aden,*
The 79th's Farewell to Gibraltar, The Burning Sands of Egypt,
The Taking of Beaumont Hamel, Kantara to El-Arish,
And, now, the world of Barke's *Scottish Ambulance Unit in Spain*
– For the true spirit is still living here and there, and perhaps
The day is not far distant when the Scottish people
Will enter into this heritage, and in so doing
Enrich the heritage of all mankind again.

Hugh MacDiarmid (1969)

He that Cannot Manage a Bag Pipe without a Staring Eye, Swelld Cheek, or wry Motion of Body or Arm had better give it over. As Slow Pipe Musick (viz the Marches) is always performd walking, it gives the Performer a better Opportunity of discovering a gracefulness of carryage in Feature & Attitude; The Bag Pipe being extremly well calculated for this, as when it is performd by a Skilful Hand & with anything of a genteel Person it is as aggreeable to the Eye as Ear.

Joseph MacDonald (c1760)

Joseph MacDonald's Compleat Theory of the Scots Highland Bagpipe
(The Piobaireachd Society, 1994)

We had the music of the bagpipe
every day at Armadale,
Dunvegan, and Coll.

Dr. Johnson appeared fond
of it, and used often to
stand for some time
with his ear close to
the great drone.

James Boswell (1773)
Boswell's Tour to the Hebrides

The fourth of April being a holiday, the sons of the mountains, resident in this province, had determined to try a game of shinty for auld lang syne. Though the weather was very threatening in the morning, the players were not to be daunted, but crossed the Bay in boats, and marched to the ground . . . under the inspiring strains of the bagpipes, to the tune of 'The Campbells are Coming,' where they were greeted by a large concourse of people, assembled to witness the game.

After sides were called, and a few other preliminaries arranged, playing commenced, and was carried on with great spirit till four P.M., when the players sat down on the grass and partook of an asado de carvo con cuero (beef roasted with the hide on,) and plenty of Ferintosh [whisky] (Aldourie and Brackla being scarce.) Dancing then commenced, and the Highland Fling danced by Messrs Maclennan and Macrae; Gille Callum, by Captain MacLellan; Sean Truise, by Mr MacDougall; and several other Scotch reels were greatly admired.

At half-past seven o'clock, the bagpipes struck up the 'Gathering' and the whole, forming two deep, marched from the field to the place of embarkation, to the tune of 'Gillean na Feileadh,' amidst loud cheering, and still louder vivas from the natives.

At nine o'clock, the players sat down to a comfortable supper at the Steamboat Hotel; and, after the cloth was removed, and bumpers quaffed for the Royal family, and the President of the Republic, Don Frutuoso Rivera, the Chairman called for a special glass for the toast of the evening and, in a neat and appropriate speech, interspersed with Gaelic, proposed, 'Tir nam bean, 's nan gleann, 's na gaisgich,' which was drunk with great enthusiasm amidst deafening cheering.

Several Gaelic and other songs were sung during the evening, and the health of our chairman, Captain MacLellan, of the ship Orpheus, being proposed, and the thanks of the company returned him, for the spirited manner in which he conducted the proceedings of the day, the whole separated at two in the morning, after drinking 'Deoch an dorus,' highly delighted with the day's amusement.

Inverness Courier (1842)

– a report of a shinty match in Montevideo, 1842

14th October – Isabella much the same, her pulse rather stronger, still continues to drink the arrowroot; her father deeply distressed, gentlemen very considerate in keeping the deck quiet above our cabin, Dr. prevented the piper playing in the evening.

Jessie Campbell (1840)

The first child to die used to run about the liveliest and most merry of all the little ones and when the Bagpipes were played by the Highland Pipers on board she would jump and clap her little hands so gleefully.

Mrs D. Bonthrow (1863)

– From the diaries of Jessie Campbell and Mrs D. Bonthrow.
Mrs Bonthrow's account took place in 1863 on board
the *Helenslee* en route to New Zealand.

Attractive, fun-loving US lady seeks occasional companionship of sincere gentleman 50-65 with car for outings, dining, dancing etc. Photos please. Pipers need not apply.

Unattributed (1990)

Advertisement, *Inverness Courier*, 1990

I will nae priest for me shall sing,
Nor yet nae bells for me to ring,
But ae Bag-pipe to play a spring.

Walter Kennedy (c1500)

from *The Pocket Book of Scottish Quotations*,
David Ross, editor (Birlinn 2000)

John Ballantine acted as a piper in Capt. James Stewart's Company in Lord George Murray's Regiment.

Several witnesses deposed, That he was forced into the Service by a party of the rebels, who took him by violence out of his bed, threatened to stab him if he did not go with them, and did not allow him time even to put on his clothes; and that afterwards they placed a guard over him to prevent his making his escape.

When the Jury returned their verdict Not Guilty, the poor fellow was in such a transport of joy that he threw his bonnet up to the very roof of the court, and cried out, 'My Lords and Gentlemen, I thank you. Not Guilty! Not Guilty! Not Guilty! Pray God bless King

George for ever; I'll serve him all the days of my life;' and immediately ran out into the castle yard, with his irons on, took up a handful of channel-water, and drank his Majesty's health.

Scots Magazine (1746)

– for an account of a piper who was less fortunate, see p25

Monument outside Sundial Cottage, Dunkeld, built by John Ballantine c1774

. . . There should be a standard set for any band wishing to compete at this level [Grade 5]. For example, the drums should have to play the massed band scores. These have all the basic elements that a drummer will ever play. Another bonus would be that all drummers would know the scores for massed bands. Pipers should play tunes that are generally played in massed bands a well. I would also like to see a rule that stops police bands from wearing guns onto the contest field.

Mark Humphrey (1999)

the Voice (Eastern United States Pipe Band Association, 1999)

First of all – *and this is private*, mind that – Piob., is not Highland music, but Italian music. See? Now. You are mad, – I suppose. Oh! rest a while till a few things sink in . . . The MacCrimmons were Christians who believed in the Simple teaching of Christ. – free from priestcraft – & Theological Dogma.They were always at loggerheads with the clergy of their day. Patrick Mor wrote a Treatise of the failings of religion as then taught, – but was afraid to publish it, as it might bring hardship on his family – It was buried with him. – Fraser [Simon] claims.

Sheanntaireachd means: Sing to Christ. See? And every letter in His name is in this word. Canntaireachd is another mutilation! It is a secret form of singing & playing by which the MacCrimmons were able to worship God in their own manner – & no one was the wiser. Sheann, is based on Genesis, Chapter 3 verse 24 as a Key in which are the principal vocables of the System, and also all the letters used in the system. The time marks are taken from verse 24.

The system is English.

A. K. Cameron (1931)

– letter to P/M William Gray. See Notes on p292.
Taken from *The Highland Pipe and Scottish Society 1750-1950*
by William Donaldson (Tuckwell Press).

Have you ever really listened carefully to a solo piper playing plastic reeds in a rubber bag? Have you noticed the lack of richness in the overall sound? the sharp top hand? the piercing quality of high A? how easily they choke? The pipe may stay very well in tune, but is it enjoyable to listen to?

I have always felt that achieving steadiness is the challenge, but achieving a rich, harmonic tone is the art. In my opinion, the combination of plastic reeds and rubber bag produce much less richness than the hide bag/cane reed combination. They can produce a steady tone, but one which sounds artificial and thin. I hope that pipers will always aspire to achieve great tone and not just steady tone.

Jack Lee (1999)
the Voice, Spring 1999

Wild cane, south of France

. . . Now, the figure 3 had a deep Theological meaning. It was considered the Perfect nonmutable System because the figure 3 could not only be divided.

Now, the Taorluath or *'Tri'* - luadh is a Symbol of the Holy Trinity and its three notes – like the three leaves of the Shamrock are symbolic of the Three figures in the Trinity. It is Three A notes on the fundmental note of the Chanter . . .

It is the Weeping Wall of the Jews till this day. Do you begin now to see what Piob., really is? I didn't dare use this information in O[ban] T[imes]. although I hinted at it. G. F. Ross advised me to keep religion out of the matter entirely, but I cannot see why, because the *truth & Secret* of it must be imposed before they begin to understand it.

. . . S. Fraser: – '664 has a deep meaning in MacCrimmon music. – meaning 3 or Trinity, as they knew the meaning of this Theological puzzle'. The meaning was given in the book of 1826. – *one reason for Suppression*. – See. Now, I tried to get this meaning from Fraser for years. But he won't come through!! The Pope of Rome has 6 6 6 figures on his cap. – Another Mystery. – See.'

A. K. Cameron (1931)

– letter to P/M William Gray. Taken from *The Highland Pipe and Scottish Society 1750-1950* by William Donaldson (Tuckwell Press). See Notes on p292

I attended the first Lowland and Border Pipers' Society competition in 1984. In these early days, many of the competitors were still trying to master the technique of operating the bellows and gave the impression of swans flapping their wings in the hope that they will eventually rise skywards. There was a difference: swans, so far as I can glean from nature films, do not beat their wings in 6/8 or in 2/4 time . . .

"But what about dress and deportment?" I hear you cry. Well, no competitor looked like a refugee from the Tartan Lads or Alexander Brothers. All that appear to be required is for a competitor to wear one or more of the following: a pair of jeans, John Lennon type spectacles, a hand-knitted sweater and a beard. Some of the more ambitious disported all four.

Ian K. Murray (1986)

Piping Times (College of Piping)

. . . This reel also reminds me of the late William MacLennan, Edinburgh, champion piper and dancer of over forty years ago, who on one occasion, when competing at a certain games was rehearsing *Bodanroshen** before his turn to compete in the Strathspeys event. The late Pipe Major Farquhar MacRae (Glasgow) (Farracher, as he was generally called by many of his endearing admirers), who had been listening, drew Willie's attention to the manner in which he (Willie) was snapping the reel and pointed out that the phrase 'Ho do ro chin' should be played round and not cut as MacLennan had been playing it. MacLennan at once acknowledged the point and when his turn came attempted to benefit by Farquhar's advice. Alas, Willie got confused and did not make a good job of his performance and on coming down from the platform made straight for Farquhar. "What's the matter?" enquired Farquhar, who was met with the exclamation, "Damn you and your ho do ro chin".

Pipe Major William Gray (1940)

Piper and Dancer, vol. 6, No. 2

* The Sheepwife

A Highland Chief was visiting an English Earl in the North of England. He took with him his piper who, after a dinner held in his Chief's honour, was asked to play. It was decided that he should play "The Lament for the Children", and the chief explained to his host how it came about that after the deaths of so many of his children, the MacCrimmon made the tune. As the variations became wilder and more complicated, the expression on the host's face became more serious and the lines on his brown became deep furrows of concentration. The last notes died away, and there fell a long silence. Finally the Earl spoke: "Would you ask him to be good enough to play it again, but this time in English".

Duke of Hamilton (1995)

As fierce as the tiger that prowls in their forest,
Those sons of the Orient leap to the plain;
But the blade striketh vainly wherever thou wanest,
Black Chanter of Chattan bestir thee again.

Mrs Ogilvie (1857)

– quoted by Diane Henderson, *Piping Times*, October 1984.

'Mrs Ogilvie' wrote these lines calling upon the legendary mystical powers of the Black Chanter of Clan Chattan to save ther worsening military situation in the Sepoy Mutiny in India at the time. William McGonagall later wrote a poem about the incident which opens in true McGonagallian style with the lines:

Twas in the year of 1857 and on the 14th of September
That the sepoy rebels at Delhi were forced to surrender.

Harsh words are often used about our judges, and it really is small consolation to reflect that stocks and drones may break your bones but words will never harm you.

Perhaps, however, we should not assume that the innate gentlemanliness of the competing pipers will last forever. It has always been our view that judges who favour their pupils or friends – and who are seen consistently so to do – should receive a boot up the backside and be barred from further judging permanently. With these sentiments no one will disagree, but when it comes to action nothing happens. The organisers let bygones be bygones and next year we see the same familiar faeces on the bench.

Seumas MacNeill (1981)

Piping Times (College of Piping)

273

I don't see the World Pipe Band Championships as being a musical event at all. It is a sporting event. You have a park with two hundred pipe bands fighting against each other, there is nothing less musical than that. You practice all year for it and you have five to seven minutes to cram all that practice in. You tune the band up for crossing the line at the designated time, and it is all about concentration and getting everyone to peak, just as a sprinter does preparing for the gun.

Robert Mathieson (1997)

The Living Tradition

From the cold North, straight to the Forth,
The Highland Clans advanced,
On Sabbath-Day made their Pipes play,
And merrily they danced.
With single Pumps they made clean Jumps,
Like Lambs among the Heather,
With Buttocks bare they did not care
Neither for Wind nor Weather.

Still South they come, with Pipe and Drum,
With their Prince or Pretender;
Whate'er he be, he may well see,
He is no small Offender.
Instead of Laws his Sword he draws,
And acts with great Oppression,
Folks Goods he takes, and his he makes,
And thinks it no Transgression.

Sir William Scott of Thirlestane (1776)

Ancient and Modern Scottish Songs Heroic Ballads etc (Edinburgh, 1776)
– an anti-Jacobite song.

MacLennan Snr.

Dear George,

The rudiments of any art are the fundamental parts necessary to acquire proficiency. It is therefore obvious that if you aspire to be a tolerable performer on the Bagpipe, you must thoroughly study the Scale, not only the nature and character of each note, but the method of holding the Chanter, the manner of placing the fingers and their position in changing from one note to another, which note is to be left open and which closed.

Agreeable performance on any instrument depends upon accuracy in tunefully playing the Scale. Your whole future depends entirely on your being properly trained at the beginning of your career, and always recollect that excellence of any sort is beyond the reach of indolence.

If you allow yourself to believe that it

is impossible for you to do what you see others perform, your despair will not allow you to succeed, but if you let a reasonable assurance animate your endeavours, with a determined resolution, good tuition, and careful practice during a severe course of training, you will overcome all difficulties.

Repeat again and again; facility will always come with diligence and labour. Endeavour to be the first man in your profession, never, however, allow yourself to become vain through success or discouraged by ill fortune.

John MacLennan (1907)

– addressing his son George (G.S.).
The Piobaireachd As MacCrimmon Played It
(John MacLennan, 1907)

MacLennan Jnr.

We have all at some time or another experienced unpleasantness or even embarrassment because we play the pipes. Perhaps you have been having a wee quiet tune on a railway train when someone in the compartment has asked you to desist. We who have chosen the noble instrument as our means of musical expression have to be particularly careful when and where we play. It is always best, for example, before performing in a train to enquire if anyone in the carriage objects to the proposed recital – and then to throw the offender off the train before you begin to play.

Seumas MacNeill (1962)

Piping Times, March 1976 (College of Piping)

Once whilst on tour in a country which shall remain anonymous, I was approached by a fellow who played in a pipe band. He asked me how I tuned the band and I explained that the pipers blew individually for five minutes and then blew collectively for another five or ten minutes. I would then make minor adjustments to drone and chanters after which we would play again collectively, re-tuning once more before the performance.

"That sounds a complicated system of tuning to me," he said, so I asked him how his band tuned up – to which he replied, "We just congregate in the band hut and drink until it sounds good!".

P/M Angus MacDonald, M.B.E. (1993)

Foreword, *Pipes of War*, by C.A. Malcolm
(Hardwicke Press, 1993)

The Piper

Oor Burns Club Supper was held in the ha'–
Oh! sirs, here's a baur worth the tellin'–
There was rowth o' guid cheer, an' a dram for us a',
An' oor he'rts wi' contentment were swellin',
Fair swellin'! Oor he'rts wi' contentment were swellin'.

There was peace an' guidwill till the haggis cam' roun',
An' a piper cam' roun' wi' the haggis;
An' wha was the piper but yon glaikit loon,
The gomeral son o' auld Maggie's,
Auld Maggie's, the fushionless son o' auld Maggie's?

His pipes in his oxter, his face like the mune,
Oh, deil tak' his drones an' his chanter!
For och! sic a skirl he gied for a tune
It scunner'd the laird o' Glenbranter,
Glenbranter, ay, scunner'd the laird o' Glenbranter.

Then up frae the fire rise oor doverin' dougs,
Wi' een that for mercy implore us;
They think we hae ta'en an ill-will to their lugs
An' they jine wi' a yowl in the chorus,
The chorus, thy jine wi' a yowl in the chorus.

Auld Duncan Mctavish he girn'd an' he grued,
Could he thole it, the puir Hielan' buddie?
In his auld-farrant wey he sat thinkin' aloud,
An' he syne ca'd the piper a cuddie,
A cuddie! He syne ca'd the piper a cuddie.

When supper was feenish'd oor chairman, Tam Reid,
Said: "We've had a harmonious meetin',
But the epithet *cuddie* 's been flung at the heid
O' the piper; an' noo he is greetin',
Ay, greetin'! I tell ye the piper is greetin'."

Then Duncan spak' up, an' nae man we're agreed
Is in age or experience riper:
"Sir, wha ca'd the piper a cuddie ne'er heed;
But wha ca'd the cuddie a piper?
A *piper!* Oh, wha ca'd the cuddie a piper?"

W. D. Cocker (1932)

Poems, Scots and English

ha' – hall; *baur* – a joke; *rowth* – plenty; *glaikit loon* – silly fellow; *gomeral* – blockhead; *fushionless* – useless; *scunner'd* – disgusted; *doverin' dougs* – lightly sleeping dogs; *een* – eyes; *lugs* – ears; *jine wi' a yowl* – join with a howl; *girn'd an' he grued* – snarled and he shuddered with disgust; *thole* – endure; *auld-farrant wey* – old-fashioned way; *syne* – then; *cuddie* – an ass; *greetin'* – weeping.

. . . We were coming back from Oban one summer evening, and between Dalmally and Tyndrum John [MacFadyen] decided we should stop and have a tune. I went over on the left hand side of the road and John crossed to the right hand side where there is a little loch, not far from Tyndrum. The midges however were murder, and I soon gave up and came back and sat in the car. John was made of sterner stuff and I remember he was playing "Catherine's Lament". It was a beautiful evening with the sun shining low from the west and the scenery was magnificent. It's an isolated part of the road but the tourist trade was pretty busy and the cars with the strange number plates were hammering in both directions. What surprised me was that they all must have seen and heard John but none of them stopped to enjoy what would be for them a unique chance to hear great piping in ideal surroundings. Eventually however one chap heading towards Oban stopped opposite me and got out of the car and came across. I thought, "He's going to ask me what John is playing and why is he playing and all the rest of it," but in a real English accent he said to me, "Am I on the right road for Crianlarich?" So I said to him, "Yes you are on the right road for Crianlarich" – but I didn't tell him he had passed it six miles back and was going in the wrong direction.

Seumas MacNeill (1981)

Piping Times, March 1981 (College of Piping)

He [John MacDougall Gillies] came into the room where I was sitting waiting for his arrival at the table and he said, 'Good afternoon' and he solemnly laid a chanter down in the middle of the table. And there the chanter stayed. I never once heard him play it, but it was a symbol of office and there it stayed, and when he was done he picked it up and went out with it.

Dr. Colin Caird (1982)

Proceedings of the Piobaireachd Society Conference, 1982
(The Piobaireachd Society)

John MacDougall Gillies

. . . But the time that impressed me most was the night before Dame Flora's* funeral. She had asked that she would lie in state in the drawing-room and that John and I would play piobaireachd. The sound of the pipe didn't stop for about two hours, because what we did was when John was repeating the ground of his tune I joined in, and then when I started a new tune he dropped out, and so on. Next day we played "MacLeod's Salute" four and a half times, and then the ground of the "Lament for the Children".

Seumas MacNeill (1981)

Dame Flora MacLeod of MacLeod with the fabled speckled MacCrimmon pipes

285

Abair ris mata, gur h-ann a b'abhaist dhomhsa bhi toirt aoibhneis lem'cheol do chluais athar anns an talla so; agus nach 'eil mi nise nam' sheann aois a dol a chur a leithid de dhimeas air a'phiobmhoir 's gu'n teid mi 'ga seideadh suas 'na dheireadh-san.

Iain Dall MacAoidh (c1750)

Say to him then that I was in the habit of giving joy with my music to his father's ears in this hall, and that I, in my old age, am not going so to demean my great pipe as to go and blow it up his rear.

John MacKay (c1750)

– from *History of Skye* by Alexander Nicolson; revised by Dr Alasdair MacLean in 1994. See Notes on p295

Duntulm Castle ruins, Skye

August 24, 1815:- Return to the Castle, take our luncheon and go aboard at three. Macleod, accompanying us in proper style with his piper. We take leave of the castle, where we have been so kindly entertained, with the salute of the seven guns. The Chief returns ashore with his piper playing the 'MacLeod's Gathering' heard to the advantage along the calm and placid loch, and dying as it retreated from us . . . There is a little poetical tradition in this country, yet there should be a great deal, considering how lately the bards and genealogists existed as a distinct order. MacLeod's hereditary piper is called MacCrimmon, but the present holder of this office has risen above his profession. He is an old man, a Lieutenant in the army, and a most capital piper, possessing about 200 tunes, most of which will probably die with him, as he declines to have any of hs sons instructed in the art. He plays to MacLeod and his Lady, but only in the same room, and maintains his minstrel image by putting on his bonnet as he begins to play.

Sir Walter Scott (1815)

The hopeless indifference with which piobaireachd playing is regarded at the present moment in Scotland is patetic. All classes are to blame, and blame must be shared by all, when they stand aside and watch one of the oldest and certainly the most unique form of music in Europe die away and be lost. The Highland laird was not the big chap he once was and he has now little money to spend on anything, and still less on a piper. How many of our Scottish nobility have a piobaireachd player among their servants? Can good piping still be heard at Moy, Dunrobin, Inveraray, Drummond Castle – and what of Dunvegan, Duart, Islay, and a host of other places famous for their pipers in days gone past?

Pipe Major William Gray (c1950)

– from his handwritten notes, which were without title or date, but appear to be for a lecture to the Scottish Pipers Association. see Notes on p292

Angus [Cameron] was the best piper in his day, and, when only eighteen, gained the competition prize at Edinburgh [July 1794] . . . Though giving great praise to old rivals, and to young aspirants, he bemoaned the general decline of the art, for he said that there was not now one single 'real piper – a man who made the pipe his business', in the whole of Appin. I suggested that it was probably owing to the want of county militia regiments, for the Highland colonels used to take their pipers with them. But he eschewed this, saying that we had plenty of pipers long before the militia was heard of. I then suggested the want of training. 'Ay! there's a deal in that, for it does tak edication! a deal o' edication'. But then, why were they 'no edicated'? So he hit it on the very head, by saying it was the decline of chieftains, and their castles and gatherings. 'Yes', said I, 'few of them live at home now'. 'At hame! ou, they're a' deed! an' they're a' puir! an' they're a' English!'.

Henry Cockburn (1841)

Taken from *The Highland Pipe and Scottish Society 1750-1950*
by William Donaldson (Tuckwell Press 2000)

Epitaph

And when on death's cold bier I'm laid
Let pipers round me serenade
And wrap me in a Highland plaid
For sheet and shroud
And o'er my grave be tribute paid
One piobaireachd loud

Unknown

Notes

- **Page 44, 83, 88, 136, 237, 240, 253, 266, 268, 270 and 288. William Gray** was a native of Mull who served in the City of Glasgow Police, rising to Lieutenant. He was also Pipe Major of the pipe band in addition to being a successful soloist. He later became an admirer of Simon Fraser – see below. Gray was challenged to a public debate in 1926 by John Grant of Rothiemurchas, Secretary of the Piobaireachd Society. The subject was the 'redundant' low A controversy which had been raging in the piping world during the 1920s and '30s. Gray successfully won the debate. For more on this controversy William Donaldson's *The Highland Pipe and Scottish Society 1750-1950* is recommended.

- **Page 44, 88, 255. Simon Fraser** of Warnambool, Australia, was said to have been taught by Peter Bruce of Glenelg who himself was taught by his father Sandy, who in turn was taught by Iain Dubh MacCrimmon and Captain Niel MacLeod of Gesto, Skye. Fraser, therefore, claimed to have inherited the authentic MacCrimmon teaching which he said had been allowed to die out in Scotland. He claimed that Gesto had written a book on the MacCrimmons with their system of canntaireachd and that this book had been supressed. Many figures in the piping world were attracted to his ideas and many still are. He was a big influence of A. K. Cameron (p266, 268), an expatriate sheep farmer in Montana, who absorbed a powerful strain of religious mysticism which he applied to piobaireachd. Cameron corresponded with P/M Willie Gray who considered Fraser's settings superior to any other. Fraser's settings were published in 1979 by B. J. Maclachlan Orme of Australia.

- **Page 97. *The Praise of the Bagpipes.*** This poem – composed by the chief of the MacDonalds of Keppoch from c1670 till his death in 1682 – was made in response to one composed by Niall Mòr MacMhuirich, in which MacMhuirich attacked the pipes. Gilleasbaig's poem was subsequently the spur to two later MacLean songs, one supporting his view of the pipes and the other against it – see *Reply to The Praise of the Bagpipes* by Lachlann Maclean on page 103.

- **p61, 229. John William O'Sullivan** was a notable figure in Prince Charles Edward

Stewart's campaign in 1745-6. He was one of the 'Seven Men of Moidart', an experienced soldier and of real value to the Prince. His manuscript was brought to the UK following the death of Cardinal York – the Prince's brother – in 1807. The manuscript, essentially a narrative addressed to the exiled King James in Rome, throws a good deal of light on the daily incidents of the '45.

• p85. **Song to Dòmhnall Gorm Og, MacDonald of Sleat.** Little is known about Iain Lom, perhaps the greatest and best-known of the vernacular poets of the 17th century. Related to the MacDonalds of Keppoch, he was born around 1624 and died in the 1690s. This song was composed to Donald Gorm Og of Sleat who died in 1643.

• p120. **The Sobieski brothers**, Charles and John, were the subjects of a tune called *Sobieski's Salute*, composed in the 1840s. The brothers claimed to be the grandsons of Prince Charles Edward Stuart (Bonnie Prince Charlie) through their father, said to be the son of Louise of Stolberg, the Prince's wife. Several distinguished Highland families privately acknowledged their claims. In certain circles the company would rise when the brothers entered the room, and when the toast to 'the King' was proposed, John would remain seated and his brother would incline his glass significantly towards him. Charles MacDonnell, born in Glengarry in 1811, was piper to both the brothers until they left Scotland. John died in 1872, Charles in 1880, and they are buried in the Catholic church in Eskadale.

• p137. **I Am Minded to Rise.** The subject of this song is Allan MacDonald (Ailean Dearg) who became chief of Clanranald in 1689. He led his clan during the 1715 rising and was wounded at Sheriffmuir. Taken to Drummond Castle, he died the following day and was buried at Innerpeffray near Crieff. The chorus and verses 1, 2 and 6 are given here.

• p140. **A Song to Red Allan.** Niall MacMhuirich (c1636-1726) is regarded as the author of the history of the MacDonalds of Clanranald which is contained within the Little Book of Clanranald. His ancestors all served as bards/historians to the MacDonalds for almost 600 years. He composed two other poems to Allan, chief of Clanranald (late 17th century).

- **p183. William MacKenzie** was secretary to the Celtic Society. It seems John MacKay had let it be known of his intentions to emigrate, prompting MacKenzie to write this letter to Reginald MacDonald of Staffa, the secretary to the Highland Society of Scotland, enlisting his support in any attempt to ensure MacKay remained in Scotland. John MacKay was eventually employed by Lord Gwydir at Drummond Castle.

- **p24, 169, 171, 175. Somerled MacDonald** was great-grandson of Niel MacLeod of Gesto, and was a founding member of the Piobaireachd Society.

p151. *The Praise of Gairloch*. William Ross (1762-91), the outstanding Gaelic love poet of the eighteenth century, was born in Skye but his parents settled in Gairloch, his mother's native district. She was a daughter of John MacKay, the famous Blind Piper of Gairloch. Ross contracted asthma and consumption while young and was advised to seek out the mountain air, and so between the years 1783 and 1786 he settled in Breadalbane. The two stanzas quoted, however, show that he missed Gairloch (he returned in 1786 as parish schoolmaster). The 'John' in line 7 is his cousin John MacKay – also a grandson of the Blind Piper – and the 'Òinseach' (female fool) was the name given to their pipes by the MacCrimmons, and, clearly, also by the Gairloch MacKays.

- **P236. *My Heart is like Oceans*.** Zachary MacAulay (c1667-c1737) or Maighstir Sgàire as he was known, was – as was his father – the factor for Lewis. It was, however, the Commissioners of the Fortified Estates who gave him the job; the Seaforth family lost the estate as a result of the 5th Earl's involvement in the 1715 rising. Prior to this MacAulay had been a schoolmaster in Stornoway after a career in the ministry was halted by a charge of fornication. His mother's ancestors were the Beatons of Husabost, Skye, a celebrated family of physicians. The poem influenced many including William Ross (see page 151, *The Praise of Gairloch*), but it's uncertain to whom it was addressed to.